Education, War and Peace

The research on which this publication was based
was funded by the Templeton Foundation.

The opinions expressed in this publication are
those of the authors and do not necessarily reflect
the views of the John Templeton Foundation.

EDUCATION, WAR AND PEACE

The Surprising Success of Private Schools in War-Torn Countries

JAMES TOOLEY

DAVID LONGFIELD

Institute of
Economic Affairs

First published in Great Britain in 2017 by
The Institute of Economic Affairs
2 Lord North Street
Westminster
London SW1P 3LB
in association with London Publishing Partnership Ltd
www.londonpublishingpartnership.co.uk

The mission of the Institute of Economic Affairs is to improve understanding
of the fundamental institutions of a free society by analysing and expounding
the role of markets in solving economic and social problems.

Copyright © James Tooley 2017

The moral rights of the authors have been asserted.

A CIP catalogue record for this book is available from the British Library.

ISBN 978-0-255-36746-2

Many IEA publications are translated into languages other
than English or are reprinted. Permission to translate or to reprint
should be sought from the Director General at the address above.

Typeset in Kepler by T&T Productions Ltd
www.tandtproductions.com

Printed and bound in Great Britain by Hobbs the Printers Ltd

CONTENTS

THE AUTHORS

James Tooley

James Tooley is Professor of Education Policy at Newcastle University and author of *The Beautiful Tree* (Penguin), winner of the 2010 Sir Antony Fisher Memorial Prize. His ground-breaking research on low-cost private education was awarded gold prize in the first IFC/FT Private Sector Development Competition, and was profiled in an American PBS documentary alongside the work of Nobel Laureate Mohammed Yunus. Building on his research, Tooley has dedicated himself to creating models of innovation in low-cost private education. He has co-founded three chains of low-cost schools: Omega Schools, Ghana, Cadmus Education, India and Cadmus Academies, Honduras. He is patron of the Association of Formidable Educational Development, an association of 5,000 low-cost private schools in Nigeria with nearly 1 million children, and chief mentor of the National Independent Schools Alliance (India). He has held positions at the Universities of Oxford and Manchester; his first job was teaching mathematics in Zimbabwe.

David Longfield

David Longfield is a researcher at the E. G. West Centre, Newcastle University, where his research focuses on education in post-conflict countries including South Sudan, Liberia and Sierra Leone. He studied for his first degree at Cambridge University followed a few years later by a PGCE at Newcastle University.

He taught mathematics for fourteen years in south India, where he also held various senior management roles. Returning to the UK in 2005 he completed an MEd in International Development at Newcastle University. He co-authored with Professor Tooley the Pearson-published response to the DFID Rigorous Literature Review on low-cost private schools.

SUMMARY

- Low-cost private schools are ubiquitous across the developing world. This book explores their nature and extent in some of the world's most difficult places, three conflict-affected states in sub-Saharan Africa: Liberia, Sierra Leone and South Sudan.
- The accepted wisdom of international agencies on education in conflict-affected states acknowledges that some kinds of low-cost private schools do emerge during conflict. However, it also holds that private schools can only be tolerated as a temporary expedient, to be replaced as soon as is feasible by universal government education.
- Our research supports the accepted wisdom in terms of the existence of low-cost private schools. They are, as in other developing countries, everywhere. For instance, 71 per cent of children in one of the poorest slums in Monrovia, Liberia, use private schools, and 61 per cent of the private schools were provided by private proprietors (i.e. for profit), not NGOs or religious groups. In each country, there was an educational 'peace dividend', with sometimes exponential growth of for-profit schools soaking up educational demand once the conflict was over.
- Many low-cost private schools were off the government's radar, meaning that official data greatly overestimated the proportion of children who were out-of-school. In South Sudan, nearly half of all schools we found, serving 28 per cent of the pupils, were not known to government.

- Children in private schools typically do better academically than those in government schools, and the private schools offer much better value for money. In Sierra Leone, private schools were typically around twice as cost-effective as government schools.
- Low-cost private schools are affordable to families living on the poverty line. In Liberia, the total cost of sending a child to a government school was found to be 75 per cent of the total cost of sending a child to a low-cost private school, once the additional costs of schooling (such as uniform, books, shoes, transport) were included.
- While this evidence clearly supports the accepted wisdom about the emergence of low-cost private schooling, it challenges the assumption that such private education should only be a temporary expedient. Instead, we suggest a new approach. In conflict-affected countries, low-cost private schools should be celebrated, and seen as major contributors to providing quality educational opportunities for all. Let education in conflict-affected states be as far as possible left to the private sector.
- Reducing the role of government in education has many potential advantages. The recent history of Liberia, Sierra Leone and South Sudan shows how government education policies were major factors in provoking the conflicts. Reducing the temptation for governments to use education for their own ends would be very positive. Moving education as far as possible outside of government control could also help reduce corruption. And private education, by delivering higher education standards, can help bring about a better educated populace, which would act as a bulwark against states oppressing their people.
- Currently, international agencies tend to focus on creating, improving and expanding the remit of ministries of education as their way of improving education. Our research

suggests an alternative approach. A major underlying aim of any involvement should be to increasingly move educational provision away from government. Every effort should be taken to ensure that any initiative takes the potential for private delivery into account.

- Governments are typically involved in the regulation, funding and provision of education. Regulations can be adapted to allow for the flourishing of low-cost private education. Private-sector curriculum initiatives should be encouraged, to avoid government monopoly in an area that can kindle conflict. Funding might only be required as targeted assistance for the most vulnerable groups who are not currently served well by private schools (for example, in remote rural areas). Any such funding should go only to the families, to help supplement their income, not to schools. Provision of schooling by government is not required given the appetite and enthusiasm of educational entrepreneurs to provide schools where they are needed.

TABLES AND FIGURES

1 INTRODUCTION

The Beautiful Tree (Tooley 2009) highlighted how an extraordinary grassroots revolution in education is taking place across the developing world. Based on research from Ghana, Nigeria, Kenya and India,[1] it showed that in slums and shanty towns, low-income urban and peri-urban[2] areas, a large majority – around 70 per cent – of children are attending low-cost private schools. In rural areas, the percentage is lower, but a significant minority are in private schools – in rural India, for instance, the figure is around 30 per cent, rising well above 50 per cent in certain states (Day Ashley et al. 2014).

Low-cost private schools are generally managed as small businesses, charging fees as low as $5 per month. One of the drivers of parents enrolling their children in these schools may be the extremely low quality of government schools serving poor communities. Teacher absenteeism is rife and, not surprisingly, learning outcomes are better in the low-cost private schools than in government schools. This is the case even though teachers in the low-cost private schools are typically less qualified and experienced than those in government ones.

It is an incredible success story – a grassroots initiative out of Africa and Asia where poorer people are taking their

---

1 Also rural China, where slightly different findings pertained (see Tooley 2009: Chapter 5).

2 The area immediately adjoining an urban area, between the suburbs and the countryside.

destinies in their own hands, refusing to acquiesce in low-quality government provision. Not everyone in the international development community sees it that way, however. The earlier research had many critics. Some academics seemed perturbed that the poor were not going along with the accepted wisdom that only government education, supported where possible by international agencies, was good for them. The poor seemed to be going against 65 years of the development consensus since the signing of the Universal Declaration of Human Rights in 1948.

However, one criticism of this earlier work that did gel with us was that the research had not shown low-cost private schools meeting the needs of the world's *poorest* children. It was looking, after all, at children in countries not at the bottom of the development rankings (Ghana, Nigeria and Kenya, China and India – although within those countries of course it was investigating children of the poor). We accepted this criticism and its implicit challenge, agreeing that a powerful, indeed compelling claim could be made about the virtues of low-cost private education if it was shown to be serving the world's poorest children better than other alternatives.

It is widely accepted that children in conflict-affected states in general, and in Africa in particular, are among the world's most deprived. ('Conflict-affected' is the term used by development experts to describe conflict and post-conflict countries). So we decided to extend our research into three conflict-affected states in Africa to see what we might find there. The countries eventually chosen were Sierra Leone, Liberia and South Sudan. In the latest Human Development Index (2016), these three are ranked among the 'least developed countries', with Sierra Leone ranking 179th out of 188 countries, Liberia 177th and South Sudan 181st. All three countries are categorised by the World Bank as 'fragile' states, featuring weak institutions, poor governance, endemic violence and limited administrative capacity. Such fragile states feature *growing* levels of extreme poverty, the opposite to what occurs in most low-income states.

The three selected countries are at different stages of emerging from conflict. Probably the most stable is Sierra Leone, which ended its decade-long civil war in 2002. The second set of national elections held since the war were concluded in September 2007, and were considered well-administrated and generally peaceful, as were the 2008 local elections. Political tensions remain, however, especially in urban areas in the south and east. This relative improvement to the security situation has not yet translated into improved prosperity: as noted above, Sierra Leone ranks as one of the world's poorest countries. Tragically, as the country appeared to be attracting investment and its economy recovering, the Ebola crisis pushed everything back by a couple of years.

The conflict in Liberia ended in 2003, and the security situation is improving, although still somewhat volatile particularly outside of Monrovia, the capital. UN peacekeepers are still deployed across the main urban areas and along major trunk roads. Violence can quickly emerge out of localised political protests, as occurred in June 2009 when a demonstration outside a major hospital ended in the complete destruction of the hospital and other official buildings. During 2010–11, it was reported that the political climate 'on the streets' was 'becoming more volatile' as controversial Bills made their way through the political process and the Truth and Reconciliation Committee's activities were publicised. However, the situation is calm now and Liberia appears to be stable, despite suffering a setback with the Ebola crisis.

The situation in South Sudan is the most volatile of all three countries. The Comprehensive Peace Agreement between the government of Sudan and the Sudan People's Liberation Movement (SPLM) was signed in January 2005 and brought to an end the long-running conflict in what was then called southern Sudan. It also set a timetable for the referendum on South Sudan's independence, which was held in January 2011 and culminated in the creation of the independent state of South Sudan in July of that year. The situation remained volatile with sporadic internal conflict and clashes with Sudan in the border areas. In 2013 there were various changes in the government culminating in the dismissal of Vice-President Riek Machar and his cabinet. In December 2013, the political power struggle between President Kiir and his ex-deputy Riek Machar descended into violence with fighting breaking out in Juba. A rebellion rapidly spread around the country, claiming hundreds of thousands of lives and displacing over a million people. Despite intensive international efforts and pressure, the many ceasefire agreements have not held.

This book first outlines what we call the 'standard approach', the accepted wisdom of development agencies and academics about the role of government and private agencies in education in conflict-affected states (Chapter 2). Perhaps surprisingly, in view of objections to a role for low-cost private schools in developing countries in general (see Day Ashley et al. 2014), it appears to be part of this accepted wisdom that some types of private schools are not only emerging but are also acceptable to the development experts. The standard approach is something along these lines: yes, some kinds of low-cost private schools do arise in conflict settings. However, as soon as fragile states are able, there is an urgent need for governments, in concert with donor agencies, to create a 'proper state', complete with a proper Ministry of Education and all its accoutrements. In other words, the accepted wisdom sees the rise of low-cost private schools as a temporary necessity, which needs to be overridden as soon as is feasible with a 'proper' government education system.

Chapters 3 and 4 then outline some of the findings of our own research on private sector involvement in the three conflict-affected states. It turns out that these states are not especially different with regard to low-cost private schools than the countries in our earlier study. We researched urban and peri-urban areas, as well as rural areas close to capital cities. We explored differences and similarities between for-profit and non-profit school types. We saw how there was an educational 'peace dividend' in each country, with sometimes exponential growth of for-profit schools in particular soaking up educational demand once conflict was over. We also saw how many of the schools were off governments' radar; if these were included in official data, then far higher proportions of children were in school than the government believed. And we were able to do detailed calculations about affordability, showing how low-cost private schooling was affordable to families living on internationally accepted poverty lines.

These findings raise the question (Chapter 5): why should this spontaneous order of low-cost private schools be viewed only as a temporary measure, as in the standard approach, tolerated only until a proper government system is brought in? The private schools appear to be doing better than the government alternative, providing better value for money. They are not even significantly more expensive to parents either, once all the costs of schooling, such as uniform, books and transport, are taken into account. Why would this more advantageous option be seen as only temporary? (In this monograph we assume that generic objections to low-cost private schools playing a role, such as that education should be free at the point of delivery, perhaps because of human rights, or that education is a public good, have been addressed and found unpersuasive. These arguments can be found in, for instance, Tooley (2009, 2012, 2013, 2015) and are not tackled further here.)

Moreover, when these new research findings are put into the context of the existing body of evidence from earlier and more recent studies (see, for example, Tooley 2009; Tooley and Longfield 2015), then the idea that the low-cost private schools should be seen as only a temporary solution appears more puzzling still. For, as we have noted, evidence from elsewhere in the developing world shows private education is serving a majority of the urban poor, and indeed is growing in size. And it is not confined to 'fragile' states at all. Evidence from Nigeria, India, Kenya and Ghana, for example, shows that even newly emerging middle-income countries have the same phenomenon.

So this leads to a possible new approach, different from the standard view: it suggests that in conflict-affected countries (but why not by extension to other non-conflict countries too? – a question left unanswered in this paper), the role played by low-cost private schools should be celebrated and seen as a major contribution to providing educational opportunities for all. The new approach says: let education in conflict-affected states be *as far as possible* left to the private sector, not as a temporary expedient but in the long term too.

With this new approach outlined, Chapter 5 also asks if indeed there could be advantages to this new way forward. It is suggested that there are likely to be important advantages, particularly around the issues of corruption and patronage. Three propositions are set out as hypotheses to be further tested against evidence. These focus on how reducing the power of the state in education can reduce the potential for patronage and oppression; how reducing the role of government in education could limit the potential for corruption; and how private education, by delivering higher education standards, could help provide a better educated populace as a bulwark against failed states oppressing their people.

Finally, Chapter 6 sets out conclusions and makes policy recommendations, discussing what the phrase *'as far as possible'* italicised above could mean in practice.[3]

---

3   Most of the material presented in this book has not previously been published, although three (unpublished) working paper reports giving research findings and method are on the E. G. West Centre website (Tooley and Longfield 2014a,b; Longfield and Tooley 2013). Some additional material and theoretical context on South Sudan has been published (Longfield 2015a,b), while an extended discussion of affordability of private schools can be found in Tooley and Longfield (2016).

2 THE STANDARD APPROACH

There is no shortage of advice on rebuilding education systems in post-conflict states. Coming in at over 1,000 pages is the *Guidebook for Planning Education in Emergencies and Reconstruction* (UNESCO/IIEP 2010). The Global Monitoring Report for 2011, *The Hidden Crisis: Armed Conflict and Education* (UNESCO 2011), weighs in at 400 pages.

These are complemented by a large number of other sources (see, for example, UNESCO 2000; World Education Forum 2000; UNESCO 2003; World Bank 2005; Buckland 2006; Inter-Agency Network for Education in Emergencies 2010). In this section, we'll use *The Hidden Crisis* as our guide, as it appears to typify the standard approach.

We can summarise the standard approach to education in conflict and post-conflict states as consisting of the following three propositions.

Proposition 1: *Government education is a cause of conflict.* Much evidence suggests that government involvement in education may often have been one of the significant problems that caused conflict.

Proposition 2: *During conflict, private education emerges.* Even when their nations are in civil war, parents' desire for education for their children does not go away. This leads to fee-paying 'community schools' – a type of private school – emerging during conflict.

Proposition 3: *As peace is restored, governments must 'normalise'
education.* Once peace is restored, the aim of governments in
fragile states is to 'normalise' education as quickly as possible, by
introducing proper ministries of education to do things normal
governments do and by incorporating the 'community schools'
into the state sector. International aid is required. This will now
be the 'right kind' of government involvement in education, unlike before.

We will give chapter and verse on these three propositions here,
before giving specific examples of how education policy has been
implemented in our three case studies: South Sudan, Sierra Leone
and Liberia. Chapter 3 will then take the second of these three
propositions ('During conflict, private education emerges') and
examine whether recent research actually supports the claim.

Government education is a cause of conflict

The literature is clear that government intervention in education
itself may have been one of the causes of conflict in the first place.
The Hidden Crisis clearly sets out this case (UNESCO 2011: 16):

> Education is seldom a primary cause of conflict. Yet it is often an
> underlying element in the political dynamic pushing countries
> towards violence. Intra-state armed conflict is often associated
> with grievances and perceived injustices linked to identity, faith,
> ethnicity and region. Education can make a difference in all
> these areas, tipping the balance in favour of peace – or conflict.

It is also articulated, in case of any doubt, how it is *government*
policy concerning education that is the problem here (ibid.: 160):

> The role of education in contributing to the conditions for armed
> conflict has received little systematic attention on the part of

governments and aid donors ... That oversight is worrying ... [as] this is an area in which policy choices have immediate consequences. There are many spheres of public policy in which government choices have little impact in the short run, but education is not one of them. What is taught in school, how it is taught and how education is financed and delivered are all policy areas in which government decisions have both an early and lasting impact, for better or for worse.

There are three areas in which 'education can make societies more prone to armed conflict'. Firstly, there is the problem when governments have provided 'too little education' (ibid.: 16):

> When large numbers of young people are denied access to decent quality basic education, the resulting poverty, unemployment and sense of hopelessness can act as forceful recruiting agents for armed militia.

Secondly, there is the problem of governments creating 'unequal access to education' (ibid.: 16):

> If education policy is seen by disadvantaged groups as a source of diminished life chances for their children, it is likely to generate a deep sense of injustice that can call into question the legitimacy of the state itself.

The report gives the example of Liberia, where the Truth and Reconciliation Commission concluded that 'limiting educational opportunities through political and social systems based on privilege, patronage and politicization was a potent source of violence' (ibid.: 16). Similarly in Côte d'Ivoire, 'resentment over the poor state of education in northern areas figured in the political mobilization leading up to the 2002–2004 civil war' (ibid.: 17).

Thirdly, there is the problem when governments promote the 'wrong type of education'. That is, governments can actively use 'school systems to reinforce prejudice and intolerance' (ibid.: 17):

> In several armed conflicts, education has been actively used to reinforce political domination, the subordination of marginalized groups and ethnic segregation. The use of education systems to foster hatred and bigotry has contributed to the underlying causes of violence in conflicts from Rwanda to Sri Lanka. And in many countries, schools have become a flashpoint in wider conflicts over cultural identity.

Government education can lead to textbooks 'explicitly or implicitly' disparaging certain social or tribal groups, reinforcing 'social divisions' (ibid.: 160). For instance, in 1983 the Sudanese government 'revived the Arabized-Islamised education system for all schools in Sudan', which southern Sudanese described as 'a deliberate act of aggression towards their culture, values and languages'. One-third of all Sudanese were not Muslim (Sommers 2005: 36). Southern Sudanese educators were particularly troubled by the fact that, in the words of one headmaster, 'everything in the curriculum is built on the Koran, even in mathematics' (ibid.: 96). An example from the official curriculum illustrated the point (ibid.: 245):

> There are five prayers in the day [for Muslims]. Ahmad has already prayed twice. How many more times does he have to pray that day? In this way, the student learns that five minus two equals three. And instead of saying something in the abstract, we have a practical example.

During conflict, private education emerges

The second part of the standard approach is about what spontaneously happens in education during the conflict process, outside of any government involvement. *The Hidden Crisis* outlines the situation (UNESCO 2011: 126):

> Whether they are in conflict zones, displaced within their own countries or refugees, parents, teachers and children affected by conflict have at least one thing in common: the extraordinary level of ambition, innovation and courage they demonstrate in trying to maintain access to education. Parents understand that education can provide children with a sense of normality and that it is an asset – sometimes the only asset – that they can carry with them if they are displaced.

What does this parental understanding, ambition, innovation and courage lead to? It leads to what *The Hidden Crisis* calls 'community initiatives' in education (ibid.: 224):

> In many conflict affected countries communities have stepped into the vacuum created by the failure of governments to maintain education. Supporting community efforts can deliver quick results for education and demonstrate that government is starting to work.

Although *The Hidden Crisis* only mentions this briefly, it clearly signals its importance by having 'Build on community initiatives' as the second of a series of 'quick wins' for development agencies (ibid.: 224). What are these 'community initiatives' in education? We are told that such initiatives charge parents fees for education – 'When public spending is eroded by conflict, parents end up paying for education ... [to] finance teacher salaries and other costs' (ibid.: 224).

Reading this it seemed it could be implying that 'community initiatives' was a euphemism for the range of private education opportunities that we had seen in other countries in Africa – but we were also open to the possibility that it reflected only the narrower phenomenon of 'community school' (a full typology of these different school types is given in Chapter 3). The important point to stress here is that the standard approach recognises that the spontaneous order does produce at least some kind of fee-paying private initiative in education to cater for parental demand.

As peace is restored, governments must 'normalise' education

The standard approach recognises that some kinds of private school will emerge, but as soon as peace is restored, the aim of governments and aid agencies is to 'normalise' everything as quickly as possible. Importantly, one of the normalising things to do is to incorporate the private initiatives into the government sector. Normalising education is done by introducing proper ministries of education to do things proper governments do, supported by international aid. Notably of course, unlike earlier government involvement in education which may have contributed to causing conflict in the first place, this will now be the 'right type of education' (ibid.: 127). Even though the governments may have been implicated in past oppression, and even though they are operating in environments which pose 'immense challenges', governments will this time, somehow, be able to deliver this 'right type' of education.

One of the first things that the Ministry of Education must do is to 'Develop a national education plan', because 'long-term reconstruction depends on the development of effective national planning systems' (ibid.: 227). A national education plan is essential and needs to be tailored to the stages of development post-conflict (ibid.: 227):

> In the early phases of reform, post-conflict governments need to set out goals and strategies that define an ambition and set the broad direction of policy. As countries move along the planning

continuum, the challenge is to develop policy instruments that link goals to the provision of inputs, the development of institutions, and national financing strategies.

Governments need to make financial commitments, especially to 'classroom construction, and ... for the recruitment and payment of teachers' (ibid.: 229). Importantly, governments should 'Withdraw user fees' (ibid.: 224), as 'Removing ... barriers by eliminating user fees and increasing public spending can deliver an early peace dividend in education' (ibid.).

Associated with this withdrawal is the incorporation of the private 'community schools' into the government system. *The Hidden Crisis* gives an example from El Salvador where 500 'community schools' which had been operating in conflict-affected areas in the 1980s were given official recognition, financial support and integrated into the Ministry of Education governance structure at the end of the war (ibid.: 224). The OECD suggests that 'a key goal of support should be to speed up the move from external provision of services, in the early community-driven reconstruction phase, to resumption of public responsibility for services in the longer term' (OECD 2008: 9).

Finally, governments must not expect to be doing all this on their own, but must seek and obtain donor finance (UNESCO 2011: 20):

Donors have a vital role to play in seizing the window of opportunity that comes with peace.

(Ibid.: 230):

Countries emerging from conflict face a twin challenge in education. They need to deliver early benefits and embark on a process of long-term reconstruction. International aid has a vital role to play in both areas.

It is notable that each of these policy directives would appear to mirror the advice given to governments in more stable situations. Eliminating user fees, developing educational sector plans, increasing funding, building new schools, training and remunerating teachers and seeking additional aid from international donors are standard policy advice for developing countries. Implementing these policies effectively is a challenge for more stable governments not facing such severe capacity or financial constraints as those emerging from conflict. This advice therefore appears not to acknowledge the challenging situations faced by the likes of South Sudan, Sierra Leone and Liberia.

In the next two chapters we will draw on empirical evidence from recent studies in three conflict and post-conflict countries to explore the standard approach's second proposition about the emergence of at least one type of private schooling during conflict. In Chapter 5 we will explore further the first proposition of the standard approach, that government involvement in education may be the cause of conflict. Before doing so, we will briefly outline how the standard approach has been operating in South Sudan, Sierra Leone and Liberia.

The standard approach in South Sudan

The post-conflict solution advocated for South Sudan follows many of the guidelines suggested by UNESCO in *The Hidden Crisis*. There has been international assistance to develop a number of educational sector plans (see Longfield 2015b), a donor programme to support school construction and reconstruction, with DFID constructing 30 primary schools and four secondary schools (Health and Education Advice and Resource Team 2012). Meanwhile government education has been made at least officially free at the point of use and there is a major push for increased development aid (Brown 2012; Watkins 2013) to increase the number of schools and enrolment rates.

The government of South Sudan together with fourteen international partners set up the Multi-Donor Trust Fund. The education section of this fund has built 336 primary school rooms, distributed 2.2 million textbooks to students in South Sudan's ten states and trained about 1,000 teachers (World Bank 2013). However, many of the plans and guidelines have remained as proposals with little implementation – illustrating the problem of insufficient capacity within government. While erstwhile British Prime Minister Gordon Brown (2012: 12, 41) appealed for more aid for education (an additional US$400 million per year between 2012 and 2016), with donor activity harnessed to the national strategy, the national strategy itself did not seem to be delivering what it was supposed to. The proposed general education budget for 2014/15 was SSP1,407 million, according to the sector plan developed in 2012 (Republic of South Sudan 2012) while the actual education budget allocation for all education (including tertiary) in July 2014 was SSP622 million (Sudan Tribune 2014), i.e. less than half that proposed.

These figures show the disconnect between the measures proposed to 'unlock the benefits of education' (UNESCO 2011: 224) and the financial and capacity realities in this post-conflict situation. Moreover, there has not been significant recognition of the extent of non-state provision, which we will come to in Chapter 3, with no noticeable attempts to incorporate alternative schools into the Ministry of Education structures.

In effect what is taking place on the ground is a far cry from the policies that are advocated and even the specific plans that have been drawn up. Not only is the reality different but also the means to implement the plans, to change the reality, are lacking. There is insufficient capacity and inadequate funding to achieve the goals in the way prescribed (Watkins 2012). The goals appear wholly unrealistic if South Sudan is to follow the conventional plans for a post-conflict nation to develop its education system.

The standard approach in Sierra Leone

The government of Sierra Leone faces the same pressures and receives the same policy advice as set out in the standard approach. The Education Act of 2004 (after the ending of the civil war) provided for free education for all in government and assisted primary and junior secondary schools (Government of Sierra Leone 2004). However, while primary education is supposed to be free, many schools reportedly imposed charges and raised levies (Leh Di Pipul Tok 2006: 25–26; World Bank 2007) as subsidies from the government were inadequate (Education for Change 2010).

The official policy direction reflects the general consensus for educational development, with an emphasis on 'building up infrastructure and an adequate qualified teaching force to cope' with the demands for schooling (Ministry of Education Science and Technology 2012: x). An official government report urged, among others, a review of the curriculum to make it more relevant, the development of a policy to address gender issues, tackling the problem of out-of-school children and reaching disadvantaged children with special needs, from underserved rural areas, etc. (Ministry of Education Science and Technology 2012).

Academics exhort the government to 'make a strong commitment to changing and improving the educational system ... to help the poorest families with the schooling costs ... to build schools in rural areas for greater accessibility' and to 'stress the importance of education and make it worthwhile, such as by providing a free meal during class to encourage attendance' (O'Neill 2014: 55).

Attempting such policies is a financial challenge for the country. The share of total public recurrent expenditure for education has been high, averaging 25.8 per cent over the period between 2004 and 2011, even reaching 29 per cent in 2011. This is well above the average of 22 per cent for Low Income Countries (LIC) and the Fast Track Initiative (FTI) benchmark of 20 per cent (Pôle de Dakar 2013). Part of the problem is the weak revenue base, with domestic revenue only 11.3 per cent of GDP (compared to the average of 16 per cent in other LICs). In other words the government is already pouring a huge proportion of its meagre resources into education.

Despite all the legislation, the financial commitments and the government's 'high priority on education' (Pôle de Dakar 2013: xxi), it is reported that 'there are 30% of children of primary school-going age still out of school' (Ministry of Education Science and Technology 2007) and net primary enrolment seems to 'have levelled off at between 62 and 69 percent' (Government of Sierra Leone 2010: 4). These figures suggest that progress has stalled since the end of the civil war and perhaps indicate that the government is not in a position to complete the task by using more of the same strategies with its limited resources.

The weak provision of government services is highlighted by the Failed States Index, where a score of 10 indicates total failure. In 2015 the government scored 9.3 for its public services (including education), placing it on a level with Afghanistan and Somalia (Fund for Peace 2015).

In the fragile and post-conflict context where the government is already putting nearly one-third of its recurrent expenditure into education, it is debatable whether further resources can be found. Even if they were, it is questionable whether by doing more of the same the government would be able to achieve its goals. The very capacity of the system to use additional funds and 'to spend financial resources effectively and efficiently may be in question' (Education for Change 2010: 17).

Indeed, the quality of learning is very poor, despite the government's efforts. An early reading assessment survey showed that 'after three years of schooling ... the great majority of children does not master the alphabet correctly or understand how it works ... children show great difficulty in reading simple words' (Pôle de Dakar 2013: 64). In addition the West African Senior School Certificate (WASSCE) pass rates for Sierra Leonean students are less than half those of Ghanaian students in English and one-seventh in mathematics. (On average 14.2 per cent passed English and 3.6 per cent passed mathematics between 2007 and 2009 (ibid.).)

The standard approach in Liberia

Liberia faces similar challenges, has been given similar recommendations and, until now, has embraced similar policies in its efforts to extend and improve education across the country. Various international agencies (including the World Bank, INEE, UNESCO, UNICEF, The Fast Track Initiative and IIEP), either alone, jointly or together with the government, have produced reports outlining the direction that the Ministry of Education should take. Programmes have been developed and initiated such as the Liberia Primary Education Recovery Programme (LPERP), the Education Sector Plan (ESP) and the Accelerated Learning Programme (ALP).

The Millennium Development Goals have been a focus for the country, with an extensive report supported by the UNDP (Ministry of Planning and Economic Affairs / UNDP 2010) looking at progress as the country sought to increase net primary enrolment from 49.3 per cent in 2008 to 100 per cent in 2015. The Education Sector Plan gives 'the main priority of government in the [education] sector as "significant progress towards the achievement of MDG and EFA Goal No. 2 by 2015"' (Ministry of Education 2010: xi).

UNICEF and UNESCO's Global Initiative on Out-of-School Children (UNICEF 2012) details a number of recommendations for the government of Liberia, including to increase educational expenditure, to build more pre-primary and primary schools (a total of over 3,000 new schools are needed by their calculations), to devise new certification schemes and establish and implement new regulation concerning teachers and schools, to strengthen capacity in the Ministry of Education, and to write and implement new (literacy and counselling) courses.

These recommendations are not dissimilar to those advocated by the Inter-Agency Network for Education in Emergencies (INEE), which recommends that the government take the following steps in education: to reconstruct and reform the education system, to increase access to quality and relevant education, to address the educational needs of the generation that missed out on education, and to improve governance in education (Inter-Agency Network for Education in Emergencies 2011).

The Ministry of Education, with the support and funding of USAID, has set up the Center for Educational Accreditation, Certification and Licensing (CEACL) and produced strong, input-based regulations to govern and control the activities of private providers of education in Liberia. In this way the government is being encouraged to take on a larger role in the oversight, regulation and control of private schools. Indeed, the policy efforts in Liberia have been to centralise the oversight of the private schools, reform and tighten the regulations and strengthen the policy implementation. The Center for Educational Accreditation, Certification and Licensing (CEACL) is responsible, in accordance to the Education Reform Act, for the issuance of permits and certificates for the whole country (Government of Liberia 2011). The regulations set standards for qualification, registration and annual appraisal of teachers, legislate that schools have 'fields, courts, gyms and other facilities for the promotion of athletics, gymnastics, football, basketball, and other psychological, bodybuilding and skill-development activities', require a very significant escrow amount to be deposited in a Ministry bank account, and allow for the Ministry to set tuition fee levels (Ministry of Education 2011).

A national consultation conducted in preparation for the Educational Sector Plan expressed the following views: that more primary schools should be built and equipped, and more trained teachers, especially females, should be provided for primary schools, that primary teachers should be given better salaries, incentives and housing, and that more textbooks should be procured with a view to providing each student with a set. In addition, special education programmes should be developed for those who cannot access normal school, and the scope of the ALP should be reviewed and broadened. Its own recommendations filled a table spanning 12 pages and including over 130 specific actions, with the Ministry of Education expected to lead the way in over 90 per cent of them (Ministry of Education 2010).

All of this is the familiar conventional wisdom, but it seems a huge and unrealistic challenge to the fragile government education system that exists in Liberia. In terms of finance and management capacity the government is hard-pressed to resource the education system. In 2010 the government was funding only 41 per cent of the education budget, with donors contributing 35 per cent and a remaining shortfall of 24 per cent (Ministry of Education 2010). Overall, external aid was estimated to be over three times the total government expenditure in 2006/07 (Poverty Reduction Economic Management Sector Unit (PREM 4) 2009).

The government is aware of the financial challenges it faces. Although there has been a free and compulsory basic education law since 2001, in 2006 the new government, recognising its lack of resources to cover the whole basic education (grades 1–9), proclaimed free and compulsory primary education (i.e. for grades 1–6) only. However, the new Education Reform Act of 2011 extended the coverage to the original target of all basic education (grades 1–9). Each county is required to have at least one Junior Secondary School per district provided that the government can afford it. UNICEF recognises that this means the law will only be implemented as resources permit (UNICEF 2012).

The World Bank (2010: 7) also reports that:

> serious human capacity gaps exist at the central and local levels of the MoE [Ministry of Education], creating governance and management challenges. Many MoE officials are unable to

perform their assigned roles, and some are in fact not aware of their responsibilities.

In a tacit acknowledgement that the government would not have the financial capacity to fund its recommendations, the report indicates that 'Partners should also increase their support to the education sector' (UNICEF 2012: 8). Yet this is in the context of a situation where donor support already covers 43.6 per cent of the education funding in the 2013/14 budget. (Education was allotted US$79,514,226 by government while donors provided US$61,570,679 in budget support for education in 2013/14 (Peah 2013).)

Despite the reports, recommendations and programmes, and notwithstanding the huge donor support for education from various sources, the reported educational outcomes at various levels have been disappointing. In 2013 all of the nearly 25,000 Liberian students who applied for admission at the University of Liberia failed the admission exam (BBC News 2013) and in 2014 only 15 out of 13,000 passed (All Africa 2014). Reports from 2008 show that 34 per cent of Liberian students who were tested at the end of grade 2 could not read a single word (Gove and Wetterberg 2011), while reading comprehension skills are reported as being 'virtually non-existent in 45% of students [from grade 2 and 3]' (45 per cent could not answer a single question about a 60-word passage that they had to read and no student could answer all five questions correctly in the study in 2008) (World Bank 2010: 88). These factors have led the government of Liberia to a very radical step – contracting out the provision of its schools to private sector providers. We discuss this further in Chapter 6.

Moving away from the standard approach

Despite the advice and exhortations, as well as the high budget allocations and substantial aid donations for education, South

Sudan, Sierra Leone and Liberia, and numerous other fragile states like them, have not been able to provide government education of adequate quantity or quality.

This raises the question as to whether there is another way for fragile countries to achieve the goal of quality education for all. In particular, is the focus on government provision – even to the extent of incorporating private 'community initiatives' into this provision – a sensible one? Batley and Mcloughlin (2010: 132) put it like this: 'to insist on direct provision by the state where there is very weak ability to fulfil the task makes no sense.'

Of course it might make sense if government provision were the only way to ensure educational provision in these countries. But the presence – and widespread acceptance in the development literature – of at least some kind of private schools arising during conflict hints that government provision might not be the only way forward. As we noted in the introduction, it is certainly not the case that government provision is the only way forward in far more stable states, such as Ghana, Nigeria, Kenya and India, where a range of different types of private school, including low-cost ones, have emerged to cater for huge parental demand for quality education. Could the same be true of conflict and post-conflict states too? In the next two chapters we set out some of our findings from recent research in three conflict-affected states.

3 THE STANDARD APPROACH VERSUS THE EVIDENCE

Challenges to the standard approach

The second proposition of the standard approach, as narrated in UNESCO's document *The Hidden Crisis*, acknowledges that fee-paying 'community initiative' schools emerge to provide education during the time of crisis, stepping in as conflict begins and government provision fails. Once conflict ends, however, the standard approach says that things must move towards government-provided, free-at-the-point-of-delivery education systems. Advocates of this position imply that 'community' involvement is largely a response to the conflict and withdrawal of government (World Bank 2005; Buckland 2006; UNESCO 2011), rather than a part of the normal educational scene in the developing world. It is certainly not seen as something desirable in itself, only as a temporary expedient.

However, against this conventional wisdom, we can note again that private educational provision, including low-cost private provision, is ubiquitous and increasing across more stable developing countries such as Kenya, Ghana, India and Nigeria (see, for example, Tooley 2009; *The Economist* 2015). It was from awareness of this that we went on to investigate the situation in the conflict-affected settings of Liberia, Sierra Leone and South Sudan. Aware of the extent of these locally initiated, community responsive, low-cost private schools in stable settings, we asked whether the same could be true of education in more fragile locations.

In this chapter we give evidence from our primary research in South Sudan, Sierra Leone and Liberia that both agrees with and challenges the second proposition of the standard approach. Yes, it is clear that parental demand leads to fee-paying schools emerging. However, using the term 'community initiatives' to describe what emerges does not do justice to the extraordinary bounty of private educational provision that we found. Moreover, the standard approach may be misguided in thinking that these private initiatives emerge only during conflict, to be replaced by government provision once the conflict is over. Instead, what we found is a veritable peace dividend of private schools, especially for-profit low-cost schools, which emerge once the conflict is over. (In Chapter 4, we go on to explore some of the features of these for-profit private schools.)

Different types of school management

Before proceeding it may be worth noting definitions of different types of school provision – in part to avoid any confusion over what makes a 'community' school. We define 'government' schools as those managed and funded by government, at any level of government including district, region/province or state. Typically, the land and buildings are also provided by government, although in some cases church or other provision may have been nationalised.

We define six types of private provision, as in Table 1. (A seventh type was found only in South Sudan, Teachers' Trade Unions (TTUs) schools. These are schools that are run by teachers who are otherwise employed as government teachers, who operate the schools as their own fee-paying, private schools in their own time.)

A community school is one that is 'owned' and 'managed' by the community. Land is typically donated by the community, the buildings are likely to be have been built through community effort, including donations in kind, and the school management committee will consist of community members. Importantly, a community school is likely to charge fees in conflict-affected settings. These fees are not available to any one individual, but are used by the school or the community for educational ends. It is also worth noting that a school is not defined as 'community' because its buildings are open for use by the community, for example by churches, sports clubs and so on. This is likely to be the case with all kinds of schools at this level, sometimes to supplement their income or to raise goodwill in the community.

Table 1   Different types of private school found in our research

Type of school	Land and buildings	Management	Pupil fees
Community	Donated or owned by 'community' (village, district, etc.)	Community members	Yes
NGO	Donated or owned by NGO	NGO nominations	Yes
Church (established)	Donated or owned by church	Church nominations	Yes
Mosque	Donated or owned by mosque	Mosque nominations	Yes
Church (independent)	Owned (or leased) by individual pastor	Individual pastor and board	Yes
Proprietor	Owned (or leased) by one or more individuals	Individual owner(s) and board	Yes

Schools run by proprietors were classified as 'for profit'. This is not to say that these proprietor-run schools make large or even any surpluses. It is simply to indicate that if any surpluses are made, then these are available to the person who owns the school to use as he or she wants. This often includes reinvesting in the school, but could also include for personal use. Typically, for-profit schools do not have any outside source of funding other than student fees (except they can raise outside investment, to be repaid if loans, or on which dividends may be paid if provided as equity).

Other private management types (NGO, community, church and mosque) were classified as non-profit. Under non-profit management, any surpluses made are only available to be used by the non-profit organisation, not by individuals. Non-profit management can also solicit grant funding from outside bodies, which they can do in order to supplement income from student fees.

Finally, based on our observations on the ground, we distinguished two types of church school, those run by established churches (for example, Wesleyan, Episcopalian, Presbyterian, Catholic) and those run by independent churches. The latter we perceived to be much more like the individual proprietor schools than the schools run by established churches, as can be seen in Table 1.

Research evidence:[1] South Sudan

We first travelled to Juba, the capital of South Sudan, in January 2012, and began our search for different types of school provision almost immediately after we landed, in the stark heat of the afternoon. Starting near the centre of the city, not far from Bulluk, the area which hosts many of the city's government schools, we went looking, and were told that there were only government and church schools to be found. Other experts we consulted said the same thing. Indeed, that's all we discovered for the first day or so; not even any 'community' schools, in the definition above, were to be found. Moving slowly further out of the centre of the city, however, we found what we had thought might be there. In the more remote areas of Gudele and Munuki, the poorest areas bordering the city, where many refugees from the war had settled in mud and brick buildings with tin roofs that glinted in the bright sun, we found evidence of a large range of low-cost private schools.

---

1   Further details of all the research, including methodology, are given in the working papers on the E. G. West Centre website (Tooley and Longfield 2014a,b; Longfield and Tooley 2013).

We followed this initial fact-finding trip with a full search of the city of Juba and its environs later in the year. We wanted a census and survey of the whole of Juba, urban and peri-urban, and the rural areas nearby, to gauge exactly how many schools of different types were available. This included the whole of the payams of Juba, Kator and Munuki (under Juba City Council) and the peri-urban areas of Juba lying within the payams of Rajaf and Northern Bari. We followed this with testing of over 2,500 primary 4 students in English and mathematics in all schools that had primary 4 classes, gave questionnaires to children, parents and teachers, and created multilevel models to analyse the data. During a two-week period working with the Nile Institute, we had 60 trained researchers out in these districts, searching from street to street and community to community to find all schools available.

In all, we discovered 199 schools of different types, with the vast majority (nearly three-quarters) private schools. These private schools were generally smaller than the government schools but they still catered for over three-fifths of the students (Table 2).

Table 2   Schools and pupils in Juba, by management type

	Number of schools	% of schools	Number of students	% of students
Private	147	73.9	55,616	62.6
Government	52	26.1	33,204	37.4
Total	199	100	88,820	100

Source: authors' own data.

Confirming our suspicions about the use of the word 'community initiatives' in the standard approach (as discussed in the previous chapter), actual 'community' schools made up only 8 per cent of school provision with less than 7 per cent of school places. Similarly, again contrary to the expectation raised by some literature (see, for example, Brown 2012), NGO schools made up less than 7 per cent of provision and school places (Figures 1 and 2). Instead, the largest groups of schools were provided by private proprietors (28 per cent), government (26 per cent) and churches (25 per cent).

Figure 1   Schools in Juba by management type

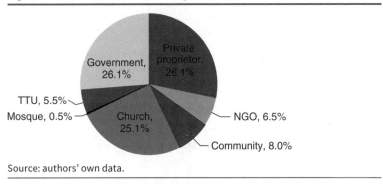

Source: authors' own data.

Figure 2   Pupils in Juba by management type

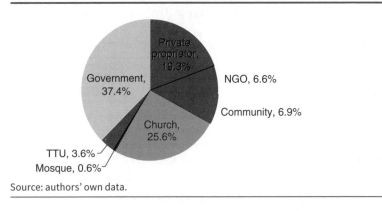

Source: authors' own data.

In Juba we found that nursery school provision is essentially private with 84 per cent of schools and 82 per cent of pupils. Primary schooling is also majority private with 76 per cent of schools and 61 per cent of pupils. Secondary school pupils are shared equally between public and private but 70 per cent of the schools are private.

These results, with so many schools run by non-state providers, might appear to reinforce the idea of the standard approach that the non-government sector responded to lack of government provision during the civil conflict by creating new schools – even if it was through more types of provision than simply 'community' schools. As the conflict ends, the accepted wisdom says that they will no longer be needed, as the government of South Sudan firmly establishes its Ministry of Education and its strategic development plan.

We asked all school managers when their schools had been established. Of course, one limitation of this method is that we were only looking at schools that were currently in existence, so it is possible that some schools may have emerged and disappeared again – such schools will obviously not register in the data that follow. However, with this caveat, it became clear that the vast majority of schools (still in existence) were established *after the conflict ended* with the signing of the Comprehensive Peace Agreement in 2005.

Contrary to the expectations raised by the standard approach, very few of the non-government schools in Juba were established during the conflict, i.e. before 2005. But the more significant point is that as soon as a degree of peace was established, the number of private schools grew rapidly (Figure 3). Particularly noteworthy is the increase in the number of private proprietor schools, which appear to be growing at a much faster rate than any of the other school types, with no sign of growth slowing down. We talked to a range of proprietors and found that many had returned to South Sudan once peace was declared, feeling that it was now possible, as educators, to serve the people and their country by establishing schools. There has also been growth in the number of church schools. Many of these are small, self-supporting schools run by the pastor (or an individual from the congregation), based in the church and serving the community centred on that local church. In a sense these are more similar to proprietor schools than the traditional church school established, funded and managed by a large national church organisation.

Figure 3   Schools in Juba by management type over time

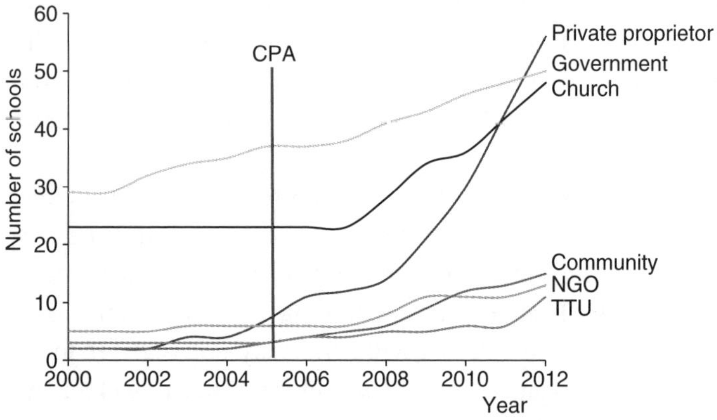

Source: authors' own data.

The conventional wisdom suggests that as the crisis unfolds there will be a decline in the number of government schools and a consequent increase in non-state provision. If these community and private schools are absorbed into the government education system soon after the conflict ends, there would then be a surge in the number of government schools. This is certainly not the case in this context. Those who invested their lives and resources in establishing schools have not given any indication that their involvement is temporary or their contribution will decline. Rather, the steadily improving quality of the classrooms that they are building as the schools grow in size (and in the year groups served), as well as the increasing number of people starting schools, suggests that this is not a temporary phenomenon but a long-term involvement.

Research evidence: Sierra Leone

Getting to Freetown, capital of Sierra Leone is an adventure in itself – you fly into the Lungi International Airport, take a battered bus down a muddy, rutted road, then take a 40-minute boat ride across choppy seas to arrive in a suburb of Freetown. On the very first day we took a taxi out of the city to a poor neighbourhood, went walking up a rocky track, and almost immediately began finding low-cost private schools – unlike in Juba, they were not at all hard to find this time.

As in Juba, we conducted a similar study of the whole of Western Area of Sierra Leone, which includes the capital city together with its rural environs. Here, working with the local NGO People's Educational Association of Sierra Leone, researchers went out in pairs to look for schools across the urban and rural parts of the region. This area had suffered during the civil war, with a reported 70 per cent of the schools in the city of Freetown destroyed. The team found over 900 schools with just 10 per cent of them owned and managed by the government (Table 3 and Figure 4).

Table 3   Schools and pupils in Western Area, by management type

School management type	Number of pupils	Number of schools	Mean school size	Std. deviation	% total pupils	% total schools
Private proprietor	41,669	317	131.4	122.9	17.1	33.1
NGO	9,821	34	288.8	236.9	4.0	3.5
Community	31,851	124	256.8	229.5	13.1	12.9
Independent church	18,583	106	175.3	164.9	7.6	11.1
Established church	56,268	158	356.1	295.1	23.1	16.5
Mosque	44,660	123	363.0	232.8	18.3	12.8
Government	30,959	62	499.3	360.4	12.7	6.5
REC (government)	10,210	34	300.2	208.4	4.2	3.5
Total	244,021	958	254.7	246.1	100.0	100.0

Source: authors' own data. REC means Rural Education Committee, a type of government school.

Private proprietors provide the largest proportion of schools (33 per cent of all schools), followed by established churches (17 per cent). Regarding pupils, 17 per cent are in government managed schools, compared with 83 per cent in private schools. Established church schools educate the largest proportion of pupils (23 per cent). Private proprietors and government schools have roughly the same proportion (17 per cent).

Figure 4   Pupils in schools in Western Area by management type

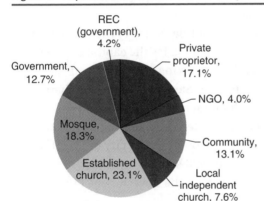

Source: authors' own data.

It is clear that the non-government sector is the major provider of schooling to the children of Western Area. The question we need to ask is whether this is a temporary phenomenon, a response to the failure of government provision due to the conflict (as the standard approach would suggest), or are these non-state providers as likely to be established in peacetime as during conflict? The data collected from the schools on their year of establishment are shown in Figure 5.

Since the civil war, the number of schools has doubled. Growth is disproportionately in the private for-profit sector: government schools show slow but steady growth, averaging about 1½ new schools per year over the last 20 years. Private proprietor schools, however, have grown at more than 20 per year in the last seven years, with a massive 1,250 per cent increase since 1990.

Figure 5   Schools in Western Area by management type over time

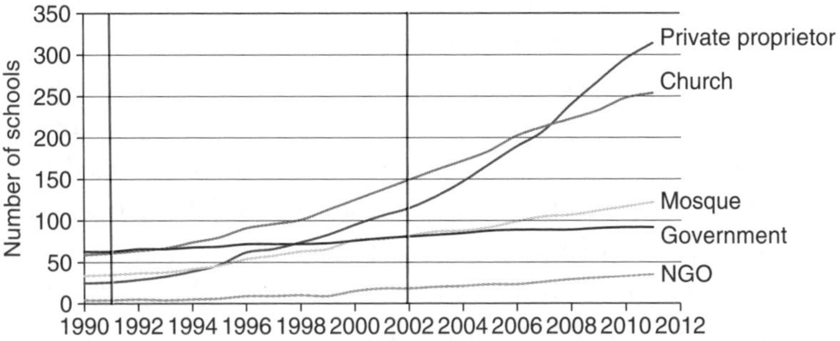

Source: authors' own data.

In this case we see that a number of the church and private proprietor schools were indeed established during the conflict (1991–2002); the Muslim community also established mosque schools during that period. Also, as expected, the number of government schools did not significantly increase during the civil war. However, we do not see a falling off in the number of new private proprietor or church schools after the conflict ended. Instead, the growth in the number of private proprietor schools appears to have increased while the growth in church schools remains steady.

Although the government has re-established the Ministry of Education and developed education plans, there is no sign that the government is willing or able to take over the schools established by the non-state providers.

The government is, however, involved in providing 'assistance' to some of the non-state schools. This takes the form of the payment of some of the teachers' salaries. During the research a number of the school managers shared their opinions about the involvement of the government in their schools. They struggled

33

with the conditions for becoming 'assisted' schools, whereby they had to forgo charging any fees to the parents to qualify for the support of the teachers. Assistance also only went to a limited number of staff, leaving the school with the challenge of raising the money for the other teachers' salaries through various appeals for donations or levies on pupils.

None of the school managers we spoke to wanted their schools to join the government system. One school which had a small proportion of the teachers paid through the assistance programme and was also receiving support from a small British charity, found the system of assistance unhelpful and was considering its future direction. The British charity wondered if the way forward was for the school to become a full government school, while the manager was more inclined to forgo the assistance, charge fees and so free the school from government control. Overall, there was no evidence of the government working to incorporate the new non-state schools into their system, as is suggested in the standard approach, and anecdotal evidence suggested that it was even difficult to register for assistance.

On the other hand, government assistance for private schools can be seen as a way in which the government can 'build on' community efforts and initiatives. It could be understood as a way of supporting those who have initiated schools across the region. This support is not primarily for the schools that have been started during the conflict; it is an earlier initiative that generally supports the older more established schools by giving 'assistance' to 'mission' schools, i.e. those set up by churches or mosques. As this appears to be the most obvious possible way for the government of Sierra Leone to 'build on' the initiatives of the people it would be wise to make some assessment of its impact. If the assistance is an effort to support and build up the locally initiated schools, then we would expect them to be an improvement on and to outperform those private schools that lack the government support.

For our research we tested 3,129 pupils from government, government-assisted and private (i.e. unassisted) schools in reading, maths and spelling, collected background data on students and their families using questionnaires and analysed the data using multilevel modelling. For our calculations here, we considered only the schools which were charging fees calculated to be affordable to the poor (i.e. low or lowest cost – we define these in Chapter 4). In each test on average the pupils in private schools (both for-profit and non-profit) outperformed the pupils in assisted schools, who in turn outperformed those in the government schools. When background variables are controlled for, the difference in reading scores is significantly lower in the government-assisted private schools compared with the unassisted private schools.[2]

Figure 6   Predicted reading scores, by management, school fees and gender

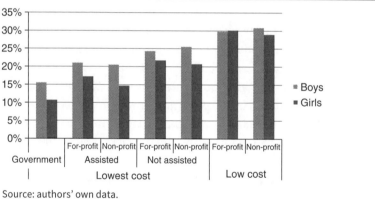

Source: authors' own data.

For instance, Figure 6 shows the results for English (reading): in a government school, an average boy would achieve 15.5 per cent, while a girl would achieve 10.8 per cent. In a low-cost private

---

2   The full multilevel model tables are given in Tooley and Longfield (2014b).

school (accessible to poor families), the boy's result would nearly double, while the girl's result would nearly triple, to 30.2 per cent in for-profit or 29.0 per cent in non-profit. Even in lowest-cost private schools, accessible to families on or below the poverty line, achievement is also significantly higher than in government schools.

Government assistance to private schools appears to lower achievement. For instance, a girl in an assisted for-profit (private proprietor) school is predicted to achieve 17.3 per cent, compared with 21.8 per cent in a non-assisted for-profit private school. In a non-profit private school, the girl will achieve 14.8 per cent if the school is assisted, but 20.8 per cent if it is not government assisted. In mathematics and English (spelling) similar results apply.

While this may be a counterintuitive finding, in that the schools with additional support from the government performed less well than those without that support, we identified possible reasons why assistance is detrimental in this case. We discovered that the schools rarely receive payment for all their teachers, so they need to find funds for the remaining teachers, but without charging fees – a difficult challenge. This also creates a two-tier system which cannot be good for staff morale. We heard that the teachers who are paid by the government were reported to be less accountable to the school principal. In addition, the payments are often made late, demotivating the teachers (Leh Di Pipul Tok 2006).

Anecdotal evidence from interviews, as well as statistical analysis of thousands of pupils' scores, indicate that, in this context, the 'assistance' of the government may be detrimental to the achievements of the schools they support. If this is the type of action that the international community is advocating for schools that have been initiated by community, civil society groups and other individuals during the conflict, then it is only likely to have a negative impact on the education in those schools.

Research evidence: Liberia

Roberts International Airport is some 56 km away from Monrovia, the capital city of Liberia. It was created by the US as an Air Force base in the early 1940s. Travelling in to the city you can readily see many private schools alongside the road, or signs pointing to schools inside. Leaving our luggage at a hotel in the city centre, we took a taxi to one of the large slums of the city, West Point, identified from internet searches. Winding our way down crowded and dirty streets, we asked our taxi driver to stop at the end of a random alleyway, and down we walked. It was not long before we found the first of many low-cost private schools.

The studies undertaken in Liberia were similar to those in Sierra Leone and South Sudan, but in this case seven designated slum areas only in the capital Monrovia were surveyed for schools. Furthermore, one of those areas, Doe Community, was chosen as the focus for an additional household survey (Tooley and Longfield 2014a).

The team of researchers working with Development Initiatives, Liberia, located 432 schools in those seven slums, serving a total of 102,205 pupils at nursery, elementary and junior high school levels. Of these schools only two were government schools, serving just over 1,000 pupils. Notably, there were no schools that were classified as community schools in the sense defined above, but of course plenty of 'community initiative' in the form of these other private schools. The majority of pupils were in schools run by private proprietors (61 per cent), while schools run by private independent churches (which show similarities with the private proprietor schools) provided places for 23 per cent of all pupils (Figure 7).

These figures show how extensive and pervasive these private schools are in these poor areas of a city that not long before had been deeply impacted by the conflict. Now, slums are usually informal settlements constructed without significant planning, direction or provision by the authorities, which may help to explain why there are so few government schools in these localities. It is known that children from slums often need to travel out of their area if they are to attend a government school (Tooley et al. 2008), so while the statistics about school numbers give a sense of their ubiquity, we needed household survey data to tell where the children who live in these areas were attending school.

Figure 7   Pupils in seven Monrovian slums, by school management type

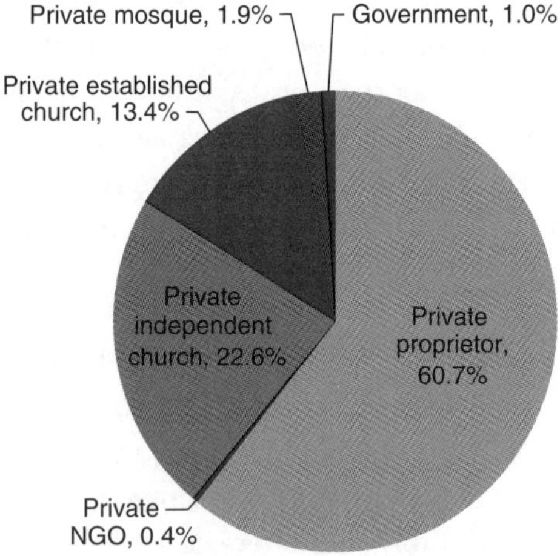

Source: authors' own data.

We conducted a study of 1,984 households (with 4,236 children aged between 3 and 14 years old) from Doe Community to explore further the percentage of children attending private school. We found that 71 per cent of the children (aged between 5 and 14 years old) from this poor community were attending private schools, 8 per cent were in government schools and 21 per cent were out of school (Table 4 and Figure 8). That is, only about 1 in 10 of school-going children were attending a government school. These figures are quite extraordinary: in the poorest slums in one of the poorest countries in the world, over 70 per cent of children are in private education.

Table 4 Doe Community children (5–14 years old) by school type

	Frequency	Percentage
Government	280	8.2
Private	2,428	71.0
Out of school	714	20.9
Total	3,422	100

Figure 8 Doe Community, percentage of children in different school types

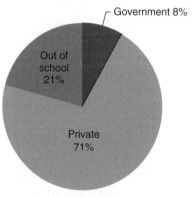

Source: authors' own data.

When did these schools emerge? Again, when collecting data for the school survey (and so with the same caveats as mentioned above), we asked managers for the date of establishment of their schools. Figure 9 shows how the number of schools has increased over time.

The civil wars took place between 1989 and 1996 and between 1999 and 2003 (see the shaded sections in Figure 9), but there is no obvious surge in the number of private schools during that time, nor indeed any decline. Again, there was a marked increase in the number of all schools, but especially for-profit private schools that emerged once peace had arrived – an educational peace dividend.

Figure 9   Schools in seven slums of Monrovia by
           management type over time

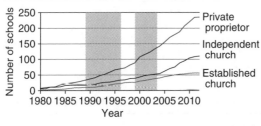

Source: authors' own data.

Research conclusions

The primary research we conducted in three fragile countries in Africa both agrees with and challenges the standard approach narrative of what happens in conflict-affected states.

Firstly, it is clear that parental demand does lead to fee-paying schools emerging, but these feature a wide range of private school types, not simply the 'community schools' that might have been inferred from the development literature. Secondly, it is apparent that private schools, and in particular private proprietor schools, emerged in the largest numbers *after* peace emerged, not during the conflict. Notice, however, that this is in the period after the conflict, when the standard approach says that governments should be expanding provision, even appropriating private schools into state service. This clearly has not happened in any of our studies.

4 SEVEN FEATURES OF FOR-PROFIT PRIVATE SCHOOLS

When we came to each of the countries to conduct the study – and when we were talking to people about our planned research before we visited – we were told that the private schools we would find were those run by communities, as well as perhaps by churches, mosques and NGOs. In the literature, 'community initiatives' is the phrase used to describe the emerging private sector, which could suggest that most of the schools would be community schools. Our research, however, clearly showed the presence of an important additional category of private school – those run by private proprietors.

Indeed, if we look again at each of the graphs showing the timeline of growth of schools in the previous chapter (Figures 3, 5 and 9), we can observe that the largest growth, almost exponential, is of proprietor-run private schools.

These schools run by proprietors, as we noted, can be classified as 'for profit', but it is important to reiterate that such schools do not necessarily make large or even any surpluses. The for-profit label simply indicates where control lies, i.e. with the entrepreneur who set up the school. If surpluses are made, then these are available to that entrepreneur to use as he or she wants.

As these for-profit schools appear to be a relatively unfamiliar type of private school in the literature, we thought it would be worthwhile to bring together some of our findings concerning this sector. Moreover, there is discussion in the education and development literature about the place of for-profit schooling, especially for the poor (see Day Ashley et al. 2014). Some believe that if private education is permitted, then it should be non-profit only – indeed, this is the legal position in some countries (for example, India). Given this, it may be worth listing a few of their more notable attributes that have come up in the course of the research. What did our research show about for-profit private schools?

In this chapter we highlight seven significant features of the private for-profit education sector (with examples given from countries named in brackets).

1. Private for-profit schools are significant providers in each country; they can be seen as an educational peace dividend (South Sudan, Sierra Leone, Liberia).
2. Private for-profit schools are not a drain on government treasuries, nor are they favoured by international donors (South Sudan, Sierra Leone).
3. Private for-profit schools are helping countries reach their development goals, much faster than they realise (South Sudan, Sierra Leone, Liberia).
4. Private for-profit schools 'reach the parts' other schools do not reach (South Sudan).
5. Private for-profit schools are affordable to the poor, and not much more expensive to poor families than government schools (Liberia).
6. Private for-profit schools appear to be fair to girls (South Sudan, Sierra Leone, Liberia).
7. Private for-profit schools are better value for money than other school types (Sierra Leone).

Private for-profit schools are significant providers in each country

The tables and graphs in the previous chapter (see Tables 2, 3 and 4, and Figures 1, 2, 4, 7 and 8) show that private proprietor (for-profit) schools are very clearly significant providers of schooling. Referring to these charts, and to the additional charts below, the following features stand out.

Table 5   Monrovia schools' survey: schools and pupils by school level and management category

		Number of pupils	Number of schools	Mean section size	Std. deviation of section size	% of pupils	% of schools
Nursery	For-profit	22,548	244	92.4	87.1	64.3	57.3
	Non-profit	12,470	181	68.9	59.4	35.6	42.5
	Government	59	1	59.0		0.2	0.2
	Total	35,077	426	82.3	77.2	100.0	100.0
Elementary	For-profit	30,757	246	125.0	108.9	59.7	57.2
	Non-profit	19,777	182	108.6	93.6	38.4	42.3
	Government	1,003	2	501.5	41.7	1.9	0.5
	Total	51,537	430	119.8	105.9	100.0	100.0
Junior High	For-profit	8,706	123	70.7	86.2	55.8	56.4
	Non-profit	6,885	95	72.4	65.9	44.2	43.6
	Total	15,591	218	71.5	77.8	100.0	100.0

Liberia

- Private for-profit schools are the most significant provider of education in the slums. In the School Survey, they accounted for 57.2 per cent of all schools and 60.7 per cent of all pupils. In the Household Survey, fully 71.0 per cent of children aged 5–14 were in private schools – with the majority likely to be enrolled with for-profit providers.
- At each level of schooling, from nursery to junior secondary, the majority of children are enrolled in for-profit private schools in the slums (Table 5).
- For-profit private schools are the fastest growing school type: in the seven years after the civil war ended they increased as much as in the previous 15 years.

South Sudan

- Private for-profit schools are providing more schools than government or church (28.1 per cent of schools, compared with 26.1 per cent and 25.1 per cent for government and church respectively).
- Private for-profit schools enrol a significant proportion of children – around one-fifth (19.3 per cent), over half the figure for government schools (37.4 per cent).
- At nursery school level, however, the largest proportion of both schools and pupils is provided by private for-profit schools (36.4 and 34.4 per cent respectively (see Table 6)).
- The largest proportion of primary schools is provided equally by private for-profit and church schools (28.1 per cent each), compared with 23.5 per cent of government schools; around one-fifth (17.7 per cent) of primary school children are in for-profit schools (see Table 7).
- For-profit private schools have grown 700 per cent since the Comprehensive Peace Agreement, an average growth of 35 per cent per annum, compared with growth of only 4 per cent per annum in government schools.

Sierra Leone

- For-profit private schools enrol about the same proportion of children as are enrolled in government schools (both around 17 per cent).
- A third of schools (33.1 per cent) are private for-profit, compared with 10 per cent government schools and 27.6 per cent church schools.
- For-profit private schools have had the most dramatic growth, especially since the end of the civil war. In the twenty years from 1990 to 2010, their numbers grew twice as fast as church schools, four times as fast as mosque schools, and 13 times as fast as government schools.

Table 6   Nursery provision in Juba, by management type

School type	Number of nursery pupils	% of nursery pupils	Number of nursery schools	% of nursery schools	Mean nursery school size
Private proprietor	4,744	34.4	39	36.4	121.6
NGO	609	4.4	6	5.6	101.5
Community	1,284	9.3	12	11.2	107.0
Church	4,678	34.0	33	30.8	141.8
Government	2,457	17.8	17	15.9	144.5
Total	13,772	100.0	107	100.0	128.7

Table 7   Primary provision in Juba, by management type

School type	Number of primary pupils	% of primary pupils	Number of primary schools	% of primary schools	Mean size of primary schools
Private proprietor	11,596	17.7	43	28.1	269.7
NGO	4,083	6.2	9	5.9	453.7
Community	4,814	7.3	15	9.8	320.9
Church	17,190	26.2	43	28.1	399.8
Mosque	575	0.9	1	0.7	575.0
Government	26,008	39.6	36	23.5	722.4
Teachers' trade union	1,399	2.1	6	3.9	233.2
Total	65,665	100.0	153	100.0	429.2

For-profit private schools are not a drain on the treasury, nor are they favoured by international donors

In two of the countries, South Sudan and Sierra Leone, we asked for-profit school managers whether their schools received government assistance. In South Sudan we also asked about other external assistance. In neither country is the for-profit sector a drain on government resources, nor is the sector favoured by external donors.

South Sudan

One of the questions we explored with the school managers during the initial interview (and which we followed up with the second phase sample of schools) was the extent to which their schools received external financial or other assistance, whether from government or outside agencies. It was reported that there was no financial assistance from government to *any* of the private schools. In the past, we were told, many private schools, particularly those run by churches, were assisted by government. 'Government-Aided' school was the term used for schools where government supplied and paid for teachers (Goldsmith 2010). However, this policy and practice has stopped, we were told. No private schools (of any management type) indicated that they were financially assisted by government now.

Table 8   Juba schools, external donor funding, by management type

School management type	The school receives donor funding		Total	% Yes
	No	Yes		
Private proprietor	54	1	55	1.8
NGO	2	10	12	83.3
Community	12	3	15	20.0
Church	38	10	48	20.8
Mosque	0	1	1	100.0
Teachers' trade union	9	1	10	10.0
Government	34	12	46	26.1
Total	149	38	187	20.3

Source: authors' own data. Note: data missing from 12 schools.

Were there other types of external financial assistance? Only one-fifth of schools indicated that they received funding from donors (Table 8). There was only one mosque school, and it received external support, as did 10 of the 12 NGO schools. Over a quarter of government schools and one-fifth of community and church schools reported receiving external support from donors. However, only one private proprietor school (out of 55 schools) reported receiving external support.

Table 9 Private management types and government assistance, Western Area, Sierra Leone

| | | Government assisted | | |
		No	Yes	Total
Private proprietor	Number	285	33	318
	%	89.6	10.4	100.0
NGO	Number	15	19	34
	%	44.1	55.9	100.0
Community	Number	69	56	125
	%	55.2	44.8	100.0
Independent church	Number	74	33	107
	%	69.2	30.8	100.0
Established church	Number	54	105	159
	%	34.0	66.0	100.0
Mosque	Number	28	97	125
	%	22.4	77.6	100.0
Total	Number	525	343	868
	%	60.5	39.5	100.0

Note: data from 868 private schools.

Sierra Leone

In Sierra Leone, government can provide assistance to schools, generally through funding some or all of the teachers' salaries. A school can, or at least could, apply to have some of its teachers put on the government payroll, with these teachers then paid directly by government. (It is then a condition that fees at primary school level are not to be collected.) Table 9 and Figure 10 show the findings. It can be seen that private for-profit schools are the *least* likely to be receiving any funding at all from government, with only a small minority (10 per cent) receiving any government assistance. This is compared with 56 per cent of NGO schools, 45 per cent of community schools, 66 per cent of established church schools and 78 per cent of mosque schools.

Figure 10 Private management types and government assistance (Sierra Leone)

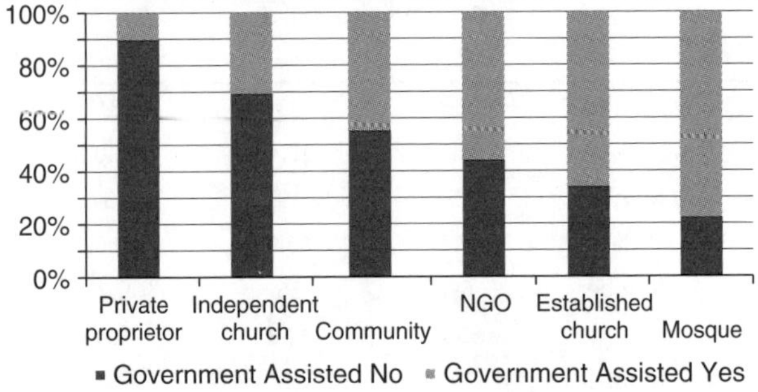

Government Assisted No ■ Government Assisted Yes

For-profit private schools are helping countries meet their development goals, much faster than governments realise

In all three countries we asked school managers whether or not their schools were registered. However, we were unable to triangulate this evidence with government records, so we can only anecdotally report that a large proportion of schools in Liberia and Sierra Leone were not registered with government. This is important for a number of reasons, not least because it means that these schools – and crucially the pupils in them – are off the government's radar. So when these governments (and international agencies) report the number of children in school, they are missing a crucial segment, those in unregistered private schools.

In South Sudan we were able to find some firmer statistics on this phenomenon.

South Sudan

Usefully, the payam offices (the district government offices) keep records of all primary schools in their area. When we checked with these, we found that nearly half (47.1 per cent) of the schools, catering for 28 per cent of the pupils in our survey, were not on the payam lists and presumably therefore not known to the government (Table 10). This is not particularly surprising, given the lack of capacity of the local (and state) government education departments. It is of course good news for South Sudan – it means that there are many fewer children out of school than they had believed.

Table 10 Invisible private primary schools (Juba)

On payam lists?	Number of pupils	Number of schools	% of pupils	% of schools
Yes	47,134	81	71.8	52.9
No	18,531	72	28.2	47.1
Total	65,665	153	100.0	100.0

We were also able to have access to the central Ministry of Education EMIS data. These data for 2010 indicated there were 125 primary schools spread across all 16 payams of Juba county. Our survey examined only 5 payams, but we found 153 primary schools in these alone. As the area covered in our research accounted for only 78 per cent of the Juba county population, this shows either that there are again many schools not recorded in official statistics, or it points to massive growth of private schools since the data were collected.

There is significant variation by management type of the proportion of schools known to the government (payam), as shown in Table 11. Apart from church schools, a majority of schools of all other types was *not* known to the payams. In particular, a large majority – 56 per cent – of private proprietor schools were not on the payam lists, and these served 38 per cent of the private proprietor schools' pupils.

Table 11   Invisible private primary schools, by management type (Juba)

Management type	On payam lists?	Number of pupils	Number of schools	% of pupils in that type	% of schools of that type
Private proprietor	Yes	7,203	19	62.1	44.2
	No	4,393	24	37.9	55.8
NGO	Yes	0	0	0.0	0.0
	No	4,083	9	100.0	100.0
Community	Yes	2,825	7	58.7	46.7
	No	1,989	8	41.3	53.3
Church	Yes	14,898	24	86.7	55.8
	No	2,292	19	13.3	44.2
Teachers' trade union	Yes	0	0	0.0	0.0
	No	1,399	6	100.0	100.0
Total	Yes	47,134	81	71.8	52.9
	No	18,531	72	28.2	47.1
Grand total		65,665	153	100.0	100.0

Clearly, government enrolment figures are going to be missing many children who are in fact at school. We were able to present these figures to senior officials at the Ministry of Education. They were delighted to realise that South Sudan was much closer to reaching its Millennium Development Goal of universal access to primary education than they had realised. In large part, the for-profit private schools had contributed to this.

For-profit private schools reach the parts other school types do not reach

South Sudan

When we began looking for schools, we only came across government and church schools close to the centre of Juba, but then stumbled across low-cost private schools as we went further afield. The results of our survey supported this preliminary finding. We were able to record precisely the location of each school researched using GPS technology (see Figure 11). The White Nile is seen on the east of the city of Juba. There is a heavy concentration of the black markers for government schools in Juba (city) payam, while as you move further away from the city centre, to the more remote payams of Munuki and Northern Bari, private proprietor schools are a much larger proportion.

Figure 11 Map of Juba schools

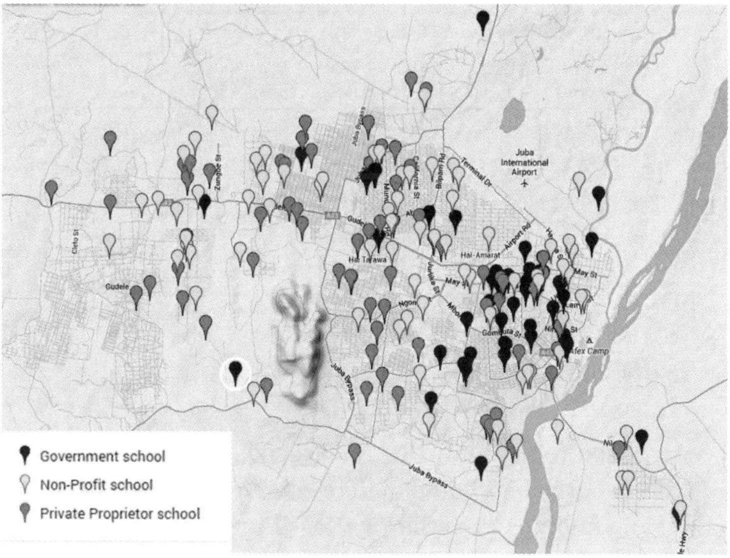

Government school
Non-Profit school
Private Proprietor school

Source: Google maps.

Different school types are distributed in different ways across the five payams, as shown in Table 12. In general, we see that the government schools are primarily in the city centre payams (Juba and Kator), with a significant proportion also in Munuki. Church schools are also predominantly in these three payams. However, community schools are spread largely away from the city, in Munuki, Northern Bari and also Rajaf. Finally, private proprietor schools are largely away from the city centre, again mostly in Munuki and Northern Bari. (Northern Bari, Rajaf and parts of Munuki are peri-urban areas of the city, most distant from the city centre.) In other words, for-profit private schools appear to be serving children in more 'out of the way' or 'remote' places than government schools, reaching the parts other school types do not reach.

Table 12   Percentage of pupils and schools by payam and management type, Juba

Payam	Private proprietor		Community		Church		Government	
	% of pupils	% of schools	% of pupils	% of schools	% of pupils	% of schools	% of pupils	% of schools
Juba	7.4	10.7	3.4	6.3	37.2	26.0	40.4	50.0
Kator	6.1	10.7	3.2	6.3	16.6	10.0	23.7	21.2
Munuki	57.8	50.0	38.5	31.3	31.0	30.0	21.8	13.5
Northern Bari	24.2	21.4	27.9	37.5	7.8	20.0	8.2	7.7
Rajaf	4.5	7.1	27.0	18.8	7.4	14.0	5.9	7.7

For-profit schools are affordable to poor families

In each of the three countries researched, we explored the affordability of private schooling. Here we give some details of the method and findings from the Liberia (slums of Monrovia) study. The other studies yield parallel results.

Liberia

Internationally accepted criteria for poverty are the following (using US$ figures at 2005 exchange rate, at purchasing power parity, PPP):

- Ultra poor – per capita daily income up to $1.25.

- Moderately poor – per capita daily income up to $2.00.
- Near poor – per capita daily income $2.00 and $4.00.
- Emerging middle class – per capita daily income around $4.00.

The 'poverty line' is often determined as families living at or below the $1.25 per capita income (at PPP). Table 13 shows these figures for Liberia, in US$ and Liberian Dollars (L$), extrapolated to the per capita income per year.

Table 13 Purchasing Power Parity (PPP) calculations

	PPP per day			PPP per year		
US$	$1.25	$2.00	$4.00	$456.25	$730.00	$1,460.00
L$	58.40	93.50	187.00	21,316	34,128	68,255

One question is what percentage of family income could be affordable to poor families to pay for their children's education? Using 10 per cent of family income (implied by one of our critics as being the maximum that such families would currently be spending in sub-Saharan African countries (Lewin 2007: 10)), we define four fee categories of private schools, relating to the four categories of family income given above:

- *Lowest cost*: those allowing families on $1.25 per capita per day (PPP) (the ultra poor) to use private schools for all family children (i.e. where school fees take up 10 per cent of total family income).
- *Low cost*: those allowing families with incomes between $1.25 and $2 per capita per day (PPP) (the moderately poor) to use private schools for all family children.
- *Medium cost*: those allowing families with incomes between $2 and $4 per capita per day (PPP) (the near poor) to use private schools for all family children.

- *Higher cost*: those allowing families with incomes above $4 per capita per day (PPP) to use private schools for all family children.

Using an average household size of five and two school-aged children,[1] we then do the calculations as shown in Table 14. A school charging up to L$5,330 will be affordable to families on or below the poverty line. That is, such a family can afford to send *all* of its children to a school costing up to L$5,330 per annum, for all fees (tuition, PTA, exam fees, registration fees, etc.). A moderately poor family can afford up to L$8,530 per annum per child, while the near poor can afford up to L$17,060. Above L$17,060 is affordable by the emerging middle class and higher.

Table 14 Affordability calculations

	Total fees per annum (L$) per child	Total family income ($1.25 PPP)	% family income ($1.25) for children in school	Total family income ($2)	% family income ($2) for children in school	Total family income ($4)	% family income ($4) for children in school
Lowest cost	5,330	106,580	10.00				
Low cost	8,530			170,638	10.00		
Medium cost	17,060					341,275	10.00

Family with 5 members, 2 in school.

Table 15 Fee categories, all schools

	Number of schools	% of schools
Lowest cost	294	73.7
Low cost	85	21.3
Medium cost	18	4.5
High cost	2	0.5
Total	399	100

Note: data missing from 33 schools.

1   See http://www.unicef.org/infobycountry/liberia_statistics.html#91

Table 16 Fee categories, all schools, by management type

		Lowest cost	Low cost	Medium cost	High cost	Total
Private proprietor	Number of schools	173	36	13	1	223
	% School management	77.6	16.1	5.8	0.4	100.0
	% Fee categories	58.8	42.4	72.2	50.0	55.9
Private NGO	Number of schools	2	0	0	0	2
	% School management	100.0	0.0	0.0	0.0	100.0
	% Fee categories	0.7	0.0	0.0	0.0	0.5
Private in-dependent church	Number of schools	84	24	1	1	110
	% School management	76.4	21.8	0.9	0.9	100.0
	% Fee categories	28.6	28.2	5.6	50.0	27.6
Private established church	Number of schools	29	23	4	0	56
	% School management	51.8	41.1	7.1	0.0	100.0
	% Fee categories	9.9	27.1	22.2	0.0	14.0
Private mosque	Number of schools	4	2	0	0	6
	% School management	66.7	33.3	0.0	0.0	100.0
	% Fee categories	1.4	2.4	0.0	0.0	1.5
Government	Number of schools	2	0	0	0	2
	% School management	100.0	0.0	0.0	0.0	100.0
	% Fee categories	0.7	0.0	0.0	0.0	0.5
Total	Number of schools	294	85	18	2	399
	% School management	73.7	21.3	4.5	0.5	100.0
	% Fee categories	100.0	100.0	100.0	100.0	100.0

Note: data missing from 33 schools.

Perhaps not surprisingly, given that all of the schools were in designated slum areas, 95 per cent of the schools found are either lowest- (73.7 per cent) or low-cost (21.3 per cent) schools. Only 4.5 per cent are medium cost, and 0.5 per cent are high cost (Table 15). Disaggregating by management type (Table 16), we see that 77.6 per cent of for-profit proprietor schools are lowest cost, and a further 16.1 per cent are low cost. Indeed, for-profit proprietor schools make up 58.8 per cent of all the lowest-cost schools. For-profit proprietor schools and those run by independent churches are very similar, with roughly the same percentage (76.4 per cent) found in the lowest-cost category. In contrast, there are many fewer schools run by established churches in the lowest-cost category, only 51.8 per cent. Over 40 per cent of schools run by established churches are in the medium-cost category.

Figure 12 Average cost to parents of government and private schools, Doe Community, Monrovia (L\$)

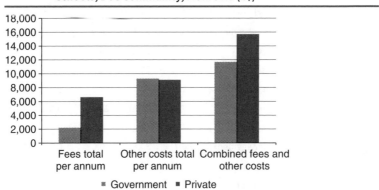

It may also be worth mentioning that our findings from the household survey in Doe Community, one of the largest slums in Monrovia, point to the relative affordability to parents of sending a child to a private school as compared with a government school. (In this household survey, we were not able to distinguish between for-profit and non-profit. Nevertheless, given the discussion above, these figures are likely to apply to both management categories.) Data from households showed that not surprisingly total fees and levies per annum were three times higher in private than government schools. However, it is also important to include the additional costs of schooling borne by parents, such as uniforms, books and transport. It turns out that these are roughly the same in both private and government schools. This means that, overall, the average cost for a parent of sending a child to government school is fully 75 per cent of the cost of sending a child to private school (Figure 12).

That is, while mean fees/levies at government schools come to $29.98 per annum, only a third of the $90.51 at private schools, the other costs total $126.46 for government schools, compared with $124.27 for private ones. Overall, the cost of sending a child to a government school comes to $159.07 per annum, not far short of the $214.25 for a private school. Moreover, private schools are typically open for longer hours than government schools. If we were to compute the *hourly* cost of sending a child to private or government school, the two school types are likely to emerge as of similar cost to parents.

For-profit private schools appear to be fair to girls

There is much discussion in the development literature about whether or not private schools discriminate against girls, or whether parents when choosing private schools discriminate against girls.[2] We were able to obtain considerable data in this regard, which supported the notion that private schools (and/or their parents) were fair to girls. For the school surveys in each country, our researchers physically counted all children in the classrooms, and compared this number to those on the register.

South Sudan

The data showed that there are roughly equal numbers of boys and girls in nursery and primary school (Table 17). In for-profit private primary schools, 50 per cent of pupils are girls, compared with 48 per cent girls in government schools. At primary level both the private proprietor and NGO schools had equal numbers

---

2   See Day Ashley et al. (2014) and Tooley and Longfield (2015) for a full discussion of this debate.

of boys and girls, while the church, government and particularly TTU schools had fewer girls than boys.

Table 17   Gender, percentage and numbers in nursery and primary school, Juba

	Nursery			Primary		
	Pupils	Schools	% Girls	Pupils	Schools	% Girls
Private proprietor	2,318	37	51	5,968	43	50
NGO	293	6	47	2,039	9	50
Community	753	12	53	2,384	15	50
Church	2,366	33	50	8,199	42	48
Mosque				575	1	100
Government	1,101	17	48	12,630	36	48
TTU				637	6	43
Total	6,826	105	50	32,432	152	49

Source: authors' own data.

Figure 13   Reading scores predicted by interaction model for low, very low and ultra-low cost schools

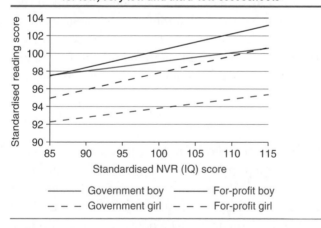

Regarding predicted achievement, obtained from our multi-level modelling of test scores in mathematics and English (for

full details of the model, see Longfield and Tooley (2013)), some interesting, statistically significant results occur concerning girls and for-profit schools. For-profit schools make a significant difference in girls' reading scores (and also to higher-IQ pupils' reading scores). Girls in for-profit schools on average do significantly better than equivalent girls in government schools. Moreover, for-profit schools enable those pupils with higher IQ scores to read better than the equivalent higher IQ pupils in government schools (Figure 13).

The different 'slopes' of the lines in Figure 13 are important: in general, for both boys and girls, in government schools the slope is lower than in for-profit schools. This suggests that more-able children in government schools are not extended academically as much as the more able in for-profit private schools. For girls, the impact is even greater: while girls are behind boys in reading in all school types, the model predicts that more-able girls in for-profit schools will actually outperform more-able boys in government schools. The same data are shown in Table 18 with the addition of (tentatively) predicted raw scores for non-profit schools added.

Table 18 Predicted raw reading scores
(low, very low and ultra-low cost schools only)

IQ score: (non-verbal reasoning test)	85 (Below average)	100 (Average)	115 (Above average)
Boy in government school	12.9	14.3	15.6
Girl in government school	8.4	9.7	11.1
Boy in for-profit school	12.9	15.4	17.8
Girl in for-profit school	10.7	13.2	15.7
Boy in non-profit school	13.7	15.0	16.4
Girl in non-profit school	9.2	10.5	11.9

Sierra Leone

In Western Area, overall, 51.9 percent of children in schools are girls. Girls make up the majority of pupils in all three categories of schools – government, non-profit and for-profit private – and at each level of primary school (Table 19).

Table 19   Gender parity in private schools, Western Area

	Private for-profit % girls	Private non-profit % girls	Government % girls	Total % girls
Primary 1	50.4	51.8	51.5	51.5
Primary 2	51.4	52.3	50.8	51.9
Primary 3	51.3	52.4	51.9	52.1
Primary 4	52.4	52.3	52.3	52.3
Primary 5	50.0	52.1	50.7	51.5
Primary 6	50.6	52.3	51.4	51.9
Total	51.0	52.2	51.4	51.9

Table 20   Gender, by management type (school survey), Monrovia

	Percentage of girls		
	Nursery	Elementary	Junior High
Private proprietor	52	51	50
Independent church	52	52	51
Established church	53	53	52
Government (2 schools only)	47	51	n/a
Mosque (7 schools only)	49	44	37

Liberia

The *School Survey* showed that there are more girls than boys in school overall in the seven slums investigated, with 51.6 per cent girls and 48.4 per cent boys. This is true at each level of schooling. Private proprietor (for-profit) schools have either more girls or equal numbers of girls and boys, at nursery, elementary and junior high school (Table 20). In the *Household Survey*, in each of the three categories (private, government and out of school), there are more girls than boys, but no significant differences between the sexes: 6.8 per cent of boys and 7.0 per cent of girls are in government school, while 66.2 per cent of boys and 64.8 per cent of girls are in private school (Figure 14).

Figure 14 Gender, by destination (household survey)

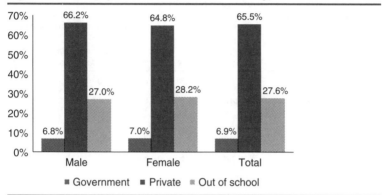

For-profit private schools are better value for money
===

For-profit private schools are better value for money

Sierra Leone

In the previous chapter, we noted (in the context of exploring the impact of government assistance to private schools – which lowered achievement) how our testing of 3,000 children across the different management types in Western Area gave varying predicted scores in English and mathematics according to management type. Table 21 gives the predicted reading scores using our multilevel modelling analysis, which were the basis for Figure 6 in Chapter 3.

Indeed, low- and lowest-cost private schools in Western Area turn out to be more academically effective than the government schools serving similar populations in mathematics too. A typical challenge at this point may be to say that these schools are able to achieve better results because they are better resourced. We obtained data from teachers themselves (in our teacher questionnaire) on the most significant element of school resourcing – teacher salaries (Table 22 and Figure 15).

Table 21   Predicted reading scores (%), by management category, gender and school fees

			Boys	Girls	% advantage over government school (boys)	% advantage over government school (girls)
Government			15.5	10.8	0	0
Lowest cost	Not assisted	For-profit	24.3	21.8	57	102
		Non-profit	25.5	20.8	65	92
	Assisted	For-profit	21	17.3	35	60
		Non-profit	20.5	14.8	32	37
Low cost		For-profit	29.8	30.2	92	178
		Non-profit	30.8	29.0	99	168

Table 22   Teacher salaries by management type, Western Area, Sierra Leone

		Number of teachers reporting	Mean monthly salary (SLL)	Standard deviation	Mean monthly salary (USD)	Ratio of salary (gov. salary base)
Government		34	443110	162982	$103.05	1.00
Lowest cost assisted	For-profit	6	326117	190162	$75.84	0.74
	Non-profit	34	371203	199454	$86.33	0.84
Lowest cost not assisted	For-profit	34	217163	136556	$50.50	0.49
	Non-profit	14	187907	139917	$43.70	0.42
Low cost	For-profit	7	253979	137213	$59.06	0.57
	Non-profit	3	193333	40415	$44.96	0.44
Medium cost	For-profit	5	366430	141937	$85.22	0.83
High cost	For-profit	1	500000	NA	$116.28	1.13
	Non-profit	1	347852	NA	$80.90	0.79

One result may be worth highlighting at the outset. Taking government school teacher salaries as the baseline, we see that only teachers in *for-profit, high-cost, private schools* are paid as much! Teachers in every other school type are paid only a fraction of government salaries.

Figure 15 Mean primary 4 teacher salaries by
management type, Western Area

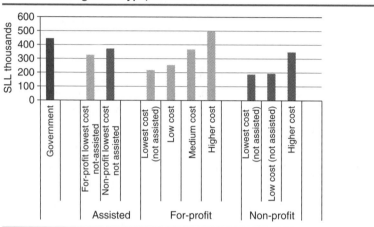

Notice too that in general, at each level, teachers in for-profit schools are paid more than those in non-profit – the opposite may have been expected given criticisms about for-profit education in the literature, where it is sometimes argued that such schools will always be acting to maximise their profits, so bear down on their teachers' salaries.[3]

In general, government assistance makes a huge impact on salaries. On average in government-assisted schools teachers are paid much more than in non-assisted schools. In the *assisted* lowest-cost for-profit schools, on average teachers are paid 74 per

---

3 The only exception here is when the schools are government assisted, when, on average, non-profits have higher teacher pay than for-profits. However, this may be a function of the way the data were collected – not all teachers in government-assisted schools are paid by government, some are 'private' teachers. This figure then probably reflects that in non-profit schools, more teachers are paid by government than in for-profit schools.

cent of government teacher salaries, but in the same type of non-assisted school, on average they are paid 49 per cent. Similarly, in the non-profit lowest-cost private schools, government assistance means average teacher salary exactly doubles.

Finally, in low-cost private schools, teachers are paid only around half of what teachers are paid on average in the government schools, while even in medium – and high-cost (non-profit) private schools, teacher salaries are only four-fifths of those in government schools.

Hence we can conclude that not only do low- and lowest-cost private schools appear to be more effective than government schools, they appear to be doing it for a fraction of the teacher salary costs. Moreover, for-profit private schools have no additional resources available to the school. For government schools and some of the non-profit schools, there are also additional resources available, such as those devoted to the government departments concerned with education. If these were added in, the achievement of private schools would seem even more pronounced.

Is it possible to quantify this cost-effectiveness advantage? One simple approach, following a method used in Pakistan (Andrabi et al. 2007: para. 5.17), is as follows. We will look at value for money with regard to reading achievement (Table 23), and also take into account differences in class size between different school management types, to work out the per-pupil cost of salary. Notice that in the sample schools, mean class size in the government schools was considerably higher than in the private schools (for example, 47.4 in government, compared with 23.7 in the lowest-cost for-profit non-assisted schools). Notice also that mean class size in the assisted private schools is nearly as high as in the government schools.

Using these figures, we can divide the mean monthly salary by the mean class size, to get 'salary per pupil'. Notice that because private schools have considerably smaller class sizes, their salary per pupil costs are higher than government for some types of private school (for example, low-cost for-profit and non-profit). Given this advantage to the government schools, the findings below are even more remarkable.

Table 23 Value for money

		Mean monthly salary (USD)	Mean class size	Salary per pupil USD	Percentage score		Cost per reading per cent		Value for money	
					Boys	Girls	Boys	Girls	Boys	Girls
Government		103.05	47.4	2.2	16	11	0.14	0.20	1.0	1.0
Lowest cost assisted	For-profit	75.84	42.8	1.8	21	17	0.09	0.10	1.7	2.0
	Non-profit	86.33	41.3	2.1	21	15	0.10	0.14	1.4	1.4
Lowest cost not assisted	For-profit	50.50	23.7	2.1	24	22	0.09	0.10	1.6	2.1
	Non-profit	43.70	25.2	1.7	26	21	0.07	0.08	2.1	2.5
Low cost	For-profit	59.06	19.8	3.0	30	30	0.10	0.10	1.4	2.0
	Non-profit	44.96	16.0	2.8	31	29	0.09	0.10	1.6	2.1

We take the percentage scores for reading (as in Table 21) and calculate the 'cost per reading percent'. Finally, we can work out the 'value for money', by comparing the costs at each management type with those of government.

From these calculations, government schools have value for money set at 1.00. Lowest-cost, non-assisted, for-profit private schools are 2.1 times more cost-effective for girls and 1.6 times more cost-effective for boys. Non-profit schools are 2.5 times more cost-effective for girls and 2.1 times for boys. Typically, non-assisted private schools are around twice as cost-effective as government schools.

Two important points must be noted here: firstly, we are using the 'predicted' rather than 'raw' scores here. These control for the background variables, and take away any advantage that private schools might have through family socioeconomic background. Secondly, the private school cost-effectiveness advantage is severely curtailed because they also have much smaller class sizes. Even though salaries are typically half those in the government schools, this means salary per pupil is often higher in the private schools.

Conclusion

This and the previous chapter have highlighted some of the findings concerning the private education sector in three conflict-affected countries in sub-Saharan Africa. In particular, in this chapter we have focused on a little-researched type of school, the proprietor-managed or for-profit private school. We were able to show how such schools have significant virtues, including serving significant proportions of poor communities, being affordable to the poor and gender fair, and being better value for money than government schools.

Overall, taking into account the important contributions made by both for-profit and non-profit private schools, the private contribution to education suggests a fusion of civil society and market working together for the public good. In *Fixing Failed States*, authors Ashraf Ghani – who played a central role in the post-Taliban settlement in Afghanistan – and Clare Lockhart point to the crucial role of 'investment in human capital' in the 'formation of a middle class in the developed world' (Ghani and Lockhart 2008: 139). They argue that a 'large middle class of professionals has been pivotal' in creating a space in which people can articulate and 'peacefully resolve social issues' (p. 142). Conversely, the consequences of 'failing to invest in human capital' lead to 'an excessive degree of inequality, social mobility, and thus persistent poverty' (ibid.). The research outlined in this book highlights the degree to which ordinary people in conflict and post-conflict countries are able and willing to invest in their children's human capital development, without any or much help from government or international agencies. An understanding of the contribution made by private education brings an appreciation of its power to contribute to enhanced educational access for the poor.

Now we return to the central argument of this book. In Chapter 2 we outlined the standard approach to the role of government and the private sector in conflict-affected states. This acknowledged that some kinds of private schools would arise, but saw them only as a temporary expedient. But given their superiority in many respects to government schools, why would they be seen in this way? In the next chapter, we outline an alternative approach of seeing these private schools as a permanent part of the educational landscape, and outline some advantages of this approach.

5 A NEW APPROACH

The standard approach to education in conflict-affected states understands that (at least some kinds of) low-cost private schools are acceptable as a short-term expedient, until government and international donors get their acts together to provide universal government schooling. Thereafter they become obsolete. However, in the last two chapters we saw how low-cost private schools, both for-profit and non-profit, provide schooling which is of a higher quality than that provided by government. Private schools are better value for money. They are affordable to poor parents. Indeed, the cost to parents of sending a child to a low-cost private school is not much more than the cost of sending a child to a government school. Private schools also appear to be fair to girls, and serve communities not reached by government. What is there not to like?

Moreover, we can bring in the evidence from elsewhere in the developing world of the ubiquity of low-cost private schools (see Tooley 2009; Tooley and Longfield 2015) and remind ourselves that this is not a temporary phenomenon that only occurs when nations are going through or recovering from conflict. Focusing only on countries of priority interest to DFID, for instance, a recent 'rigorous literature review' showed low-cost private schools in India, Pakistan, Bangladesh, Nepal, Nigeria, Kenya, Tanzania, Ghana, South Africa, Malawi and Jamaica. Low-cost private schools are a standard feature of education throughout the developing world.

With this reminder, we can construct an alternative argument outlining a new approach to the role of private schooling in 'fragile', conflict-affected states. (Some might wonder if it perhaps has wider application to other countries too. The argument here focuses only on the case of fragile countries, with this question left open.) The 'new approach' has five premises:

- There are roles that governments in fragile, conflict-affected states need to provide urgently. These include internal and external security, establishing the rule of law, tackling corruption, and establishing democratic institutions.

- Educational entrepreneurs, in both for-profit and non-profit sectors, have shown that they are able and willing to provide educational opportunities – including for the poor – that are superior to government provision in terms of achievement and value for money, and have many other beneficial characteristics, such as affordability and gender fairness. Government assistance to private schools seems to have a negative impact.

- These educational entrepreneurs have particularly stepped in *after* conflict has ended, so provide an educational peace dividend.

- In other non-fragile developing countries we also see that low-cost private school provision exists in large numbers, showing that it has stability and demonstrating enduring capability.

- Therefore, the standard approach to low-cost private schools in conflict-affected states is not sensible. Private schools should be embraced as an important – and not temporary – part of any solution to educational problems in such states. The role of government in education does not have to be extended, as in the standard approach, but instead can be systematically reduced.

In other words, there is no need to overburden a fragile government with the extra challenges of providing schooling for all when there are others who are already actively educating children. There are plenty of entrepreneurs who are willing to provide educational opportunities. There are also far more press-ing tasks for governments to be engaged in. The new approach says: let education in conflict-affected countries be left to the private sector *as much as is possible.*

The italicised phrase will be discussed in Chapter 6, where outline policy proposals are indicated. Clearly, one of the areas of concern will be rural areas. Our primary research only covered rural areas near to capital cities, which may not be representative of other rural areas. The findings from urban areas parallel find-ings for urban areas in countries such as Nigeria, Ghana, Kenya and India. Of these, only India has good data on rural private school enrolment, where the figure is now around 30 per cent, in-creasing annually. Given the similarities with the urban data, it may be that a similar proportion of children in rural areas would also be found in private schools in the three countries surveyed. If so, we will need to consider how to assist the 70 per cent of rural children who are not in private schools.

It is clear that this new approach could bring several clear ben-efits. By reducing the involvement of government in education in conflict-affected states, we suggest that the following three advantages could emerge (these are in the form of propositions requiring further evidence, although some indicative evidence is given later; perhaps the third proposition is the most important):

Proposition 1: By reducing the involvement of government in edu-cation, we reduce the size of government overall and hence the potential for corruption.

Proposition 2: A better educated populace is one bulwark against failed states oppressing their people. Evidence shows that the private sector is better able than governments to deliver superior educational standards.

Proposition 3: If the power of the state in education can be reduced, then it will decrease the potential for patronage with groups using (or withholding) government education for oppressive means.

The reasoning behind the first and second propositions can be fairly easily outlined.

Reducing the involvement of the state in education can reduce corruption

Regarding Proposition 1, corruption is a hugely significant problem in fragile and post-conflict states. In the corruption perceptions index, where the country judged least corrupt is ranked 1st, South Sudan is ranked 163rd out of 167 countries, only ahead of Afghanistan, Iraq, Libya and Somalia. Sierra Leone is 119th, while Liberia is 83rd (Transparency International 2015). Education is also a significant part of the budgets in these countries. For instance, expenditure on education as a percentage of total government expenditure, including transfers from international agencies, was estimated at 29.1 per cent for Sierra Leone in 2011 (MoFED 2012).

Putting these two facts together, it could be argued that removing education from government budgets, as far as possible, would reduce the potential for corruption at a multitude of levels. For instance, the teachers who feel obliged to use 'influence' to short-circuit the system (in order to get their names on the government books), the ghost teachers on the government payroll, and the head teachers who inflate the number on the roll to increase the government subsidies paid to their schools, could all be reduced (Leh Di Pipul Tok 2006).

Education is not immune from corrupt practices related to rent seeking, with education officials, for example, selling government teaching posts for bribes (*Express Tribune* 2012; Khatete and Asiago 2013; *Swazi Observer* 2015). Removing a considerable proportion of the total government expenditure that goes on education will reduce the opportunity for corruption and at the same time free up resources for other essential services of government, including promoting the rule of law.

Better education delivered by the private sector can be one bulwark against oppression

We need good quality education in conflict-affected countries to avoid a return to conflict. The World Bank notes that 'Education that helps to build stronger resilience to conflict is therefore a critical strategy for postconflict reconstruction' (World Bank 2005: xv). The EFA Global Monitoring Report (UNESCO 2011: 3) notes that:

> '*The combination of a "youth bulge" and failures in education represent a risk of conflict.* Education systems in many conflict-affected countries are not providing youth with the skills they need to escape poverty and unemployment. With over 60 per cent of the population in many conflict-affected countries aged under 25, education of good quality is critical to overcoming the economic despair that often contributes to violent conflict [emphasis in the original].'

But across the developing world private education has been shown to be better able to deliver 'education of good quality' than government provision (Bold et al. 2013; Day Ashley et al. 2014; Tooley and Longfield 2015; Tooley 2016). Hence, allowing a much greater role for the private sector in education may be the easiest and quickest way for a government in a post-conflict situation to improve educational quality for its population.

Reducing the power of the state in education reduces opportunities for oppression

The third proposition is perhaps the most interesting and challenging. We already noted the acceptance under the standard approach that government education itself may have been responsible for some conflicts, either through providing the 'wrong type' of education, which oppresses groups, or by not providing enough education. There is always a danger, particularly in failed states, that those in power may resort to patronage or oppression. Indeed, the OECD reports that education appears to be one of the services most prone to 'polarisation and manipulation' (OECD 2008: 9). If the government's power over education can be reduced, then the potential to use it for harm can be minimised. In this section we want to test this hypothesis against historical research. 'The iron law of oligarchy' might be a useful concept with which to explore this phenomenon.

The iron law of oligarchy

In *Why Nations Fail*, Acemoglu and Robinson (2013) point to the concept of the 'iron law of oligarchy'. 'History', they note, 'is full of examples of revolutions and radical movements replacing one tyranny with another'. In many cases in sub-Saharan Africa and Asia, post-independence governments simply (ibid.: 111–13)

> repeated and intensified the abuses of their predecessors, often severely narrowing the distribution of political power, dismantling constraints, and undermining the already meagre incentives that economic institutions provided for investment and economic progress.

One of the examples given is of railways in Sierra Leone. In 1898, there was a rebellion against the British levying of a hut tax. This was strongest in the south, in Mendeland. The hut tax rebellion was put down, but this led to the need to control the newly opening up hinterland. The British had started a railway from Freetown in March 1896, but now they went for a different route, not going northeast as planned but going south into Mendeland, which had been 'the heart of the rebellion' (ibid.: 336). In other words, the British developed the railway in Sierra Leone to assert political and military power, not in order to develop the protectorate economically, as intended with the original route.

But the railway was also a source of contention after Sierra Leone achieved 'independence' in 1961. The problems started with the government of the All People's Congress Party (APC) led by Siaka Stevens in 1967. Stevens was from the north, from where his party also received most support. The railway, recall, went south – and by this time it *was* fulfilling an economic role, transporting coffee and cocoa, even diamonds. The people in the south, especially those in Mendeland, had supported the opposition, not Siaka Stevens. Acemoglu and Robinson (ibid.: 337) summarise what Stevens did next:

> so he pulled up the railway line to Mendeland. He then went ahead and sold off the track and rolling stock to make the change as irreversible as possible. ... There are no more trains to Bo.

This inflicted fatal damage on Sierra Leone's economy:

> But like many of Africa's postindependence leaders, when the choice was between consolidating power and encouraging economic growth, Stevens chose consolidating his power, and he never looked back. Today you can't take the train to Bo anymore, because like Tsar Nicholas I, who feared that the railways would bring revolution to Russia, Stevens believed the railways would strengthen his opponents.

Acemoglu and Robinson (2013: 343) give other examples, from marketing boards and diamond mining, to illustrate the same point – how structures created by the British were then replicated and extended under the new post-colonial governments:

> Sierra Leone's development, or lack thereof, could be best understood as the outcome of the vicious circle. British colonial

authorities built extractive institutions in the first place, and the postindependence African politicians were only too happy to take up the baton for themselves.

The authors believe that the vicious circle 'is so extreme and at some level so strange that it deserves a special name' (p. 360), hence the (borrowed) term 'iron law of oligarchy'. The question we pose here is whether education could also be viewed in a parallel way, and be subject to this iron law too.

The iron law of oligarchy applied to education

Changing the routes of railways, or abandoning them altogether, is one instrument that the state can use to oppress its people – whether through a colonial government or its post-colonial successor. But another way, prima facie, of controlling people for oppressive purposes is through education. If so, then one can see considerable advantages in keeping education – a potentially very repressive tool – out of the reach of governments.

It turns out that the conflicts in Sierra Leone, South Sudan and Liberia were all fuelled by the government's use of education to oppress or control the population or to exclude sections of society. This process originated with the colonising powers, then, following the iron law, continued under the newly independent governments.

The iron law in South Sudan

In this section we examine the interplay of politics, education and conflict in what is now South Sudan. We review the situation from before the Anglo-Egyptian Condominium that ruled the whole country from 1899 to 1956, through the period when southern Sudan was part of an independent Sudan, to the Comprehensive Peace Agreement (CPA) between the Sudan People's

Liberation Movement (SPLM) and the Government of Sudan that came into effect in January 2005. This peace agreement led to the creation of an independent South Sudan in 2011. Exploring these policies we see that the conflict in southern Sudan was inextricably linked to government education policies.

The Turco-Egyptian era to 1898 was marked by 'Egyptian overlords bent on expanding their empire southwards and extracting resources and soldiers in the process' (Sommers 2005: 48). There was an accompanying increase in slave raiding and slave ownership, with the south (of Sudan) becoming 'the state's exploitable hinterland' and its inhabitants viewed as a distinctly inferior race of people (Sommers 2005: 50). From the outset of British rule in 1899, the colonialists entering southern Sudan saw themselves as fundamentally different from their Arab predecessors. They arrived aiming to eradicate slavery and bring 'civilisation' to southerners.

Some writers suggest that they achieved these goals and that 'the British were associated with the redemption of the South from the Arab slave raids' with this (together with peaceful preaching, medical and education services) influencing the people towards Christianity (Deng 2001). However, Johnson (2003) points out the British also burnt villages (in response to local defiance), seized cattle (as fines) and carried off captives (this time to prison rather than slavery), all in the name of establishing government authority. From the perspective of southerners, their behaviour may have seemed strikingly similar to the slavers they sought to replace (Sommers 2005: 50).

From 1899 to 1955, Britain and Egypt ruled all of present day Sudan as an Anglo-Egyptian Condominium, but the northern and southern areas were administered as separate provinces with the British having greater control than Egypt over southern Sudan. British policies were aimed at preventing the economic integration of the two regions to curtail the north's Arabic and Islamic influence, the south being a buffer that could preserve

Christian values and possibly be developed into a separate political entity or integrated into British East Africa (Prendergast et al. 2002).

One of their key methods of maintaining power was through control over education. Not only did the British not provide or promote schooling, they also controlled and limited the education that the missionary societies sought to bring (Sommers 2005: 51):

> Education was thought unnecessary, with minimal exceptions, for most of southern Sudan. Limiting the spread of education would limit threats to local customs and so, in the view of British colonial administrators, make governance easier.

While some have commented that 'the educational policy of the Sudan government in the south was naively simple: Leave it to the missionaries' (Collins 1983: 198, quoted in Sommers 2005), others note that the British administration did not 'leave it' but rather interfered to limit the quantity and control the content of the education that the missionaries did provide.

The major form of schooling in southern Sudan for the first two decades of the twentieth century was provided by three missionary societies, the Church Missionary Society (CMS), the American Presbyterian Mission, and the Roman Catholic Verona Fathers' Mission. The missions were severely limited in the number of children they could educate as the government feared that as a result of their work the southern Sudanese might become too influential and cause problems of basic political control.

As a result of these restrictions, by 1920 there were only about a dozen schools in southern Sudan, educating around 400 pupils (Sanderson 1980: 163). There are tantalising mentions of 'bush schools' in some of the literature (for example, ibid.: 163), but not much information given. However, it seems that these schools, dismissed pejoratively by governments and commentators, may have been akin to the low-cost private schools that one sees today – set up by the indigenous population in order to provide some education opportunities. Little is known about their nature and extent, but as in Kenya, where we know more (see Tooley 2009), they are likely to have been seen negatively by the authorities, who would have sought to eliminate them.

In the 1920s there was a slight change in policy as a result of the government's dissatisfaction with its own administration and inability to subdue the Nuer people. It began to give the missions some financial aid for their education programmes. In doing so government claimed the right to further direct and control the education that the missions were providing. They denied them any real power in educational policy-making, while still holding to the principle that the provision of education was not the role of the government (Sanderson 1980).

During the 1930s the government professed a desire to educate southern Sudanese boys at a post-primary level for minor government posts. Such a small number were allowed to participate that relationships between government and missions were severely strained. The government even counted up the number of low-ranking posts that they expected to be available in the administration and restricted intermediate education to only that number (ibid.: 1980). In this way the government kept a particularly tight control on the provision of education beyond the primary level.

The government also operated the 'Southern Policy', a policy of encouraging 'African' and of opposing Islamic culture. It remained wary of education, however, concerned that it would 'divorce students from the customs of their own tribe, thus reducing their effectiveness as tribal leaders' (Johnson 2003: 15). Its policies also 'tended to discourage, rather than encourage, education in some areas of the southern Sudan, especially among pastoralist people' (ibid.: 15).

Despite these challenges, the quality and quantity of primary education did improve slowly during the 1940s, but the intermediate and secondary levels did not expand in line with the needs of the society at the time (Sanderson 1980). These events and attitudes led Deng (2006: 17) to comment:

> There is a consistent pattern in developing countries of the 'ruling elite' adopting a paternalistic approach in setting priorities for the communities. Southern Sudan is not an exception.

In 1945, as pressure came for independence and the British saw that Sudan would form a single independent country, the official attitude to education changed again. At this point the northern Sudanese were taking greater control over developments, with a process of 'Sudanisation' replacing British officials with Sudanese nationals. Almost all colonial administrators were removed between June and November 1954 (Prendergast et al. 2002), and the Khartoum government saw Arabic and the Islamisation of the south as a natural corollary of Sudan's political independence (Sanderson 1980). The British also recognised the need for the south to catch up educationally and economically with the north. However, it was too late to effect any significant educational change or major socioeconomic development before the country was granted independence in January 1956 (Deng 2006). At that point power was handed from Britain to the northern Arab elites, with the southerners resenting the policies that had relegated them to an inferior position (Deng 1995), feeling betrayed as they were handed over to what they felt was a new northern colonial power (Deng 2006).

The huge difference between northern and southern Sudan in terms of their educational development can be seen in Table 24, which shows that the south, with 28 per cent of the population, had less than 10 per cent of the educational provision in all levels apart from Commercial Secondary Schools (where there were only three in the whole of Sudan, one in the south). The south had under 9 secondary schools per million population, while the north had 42 per million (almost five times as many).

Table 24   Educational provision and access in
North and South Sudan in 1960

Number of education facilities (streams, schools and universities)					
Level of education	North		South		Total
Intermediate streams (Boys)	194	91%	20	9%	214
Intermediate streams (Girls)	55	98%	1	2%	56
Secondary streams (Boys)	49	96%	2	4%	51
Secondary streams (Girls)	14	100%	0	0%	14
Commercial secondary schools	2	67%	1	33%	3
Technical secondary schools	3	100%	0	0%	3
Universities	4	100%	0	0%	4
Khartoum University students	1,156	95%	60	5%	1,216
Population Census in 1956 (000)	7,480	72%	2,783	28%	10,263

Source: Deng (2006: 5, Table 2.1), using data from Oduho and Deng (1963).

While post-colonial reflections are generally positive about the British accomplishments in Sudan, they are critical of the lack of development under the Southern Policy. Paul Howell, who had served in southern Sudan, observed that 'one of the biggest [British] errors was ... the scandalous lack of investment in development and education in the south' (quoted in Deng 1995: 96). Southern Sudan entered the period of Sudanese independence with a weak education system, an uneducated population and few sufficiently qualified for high office (Sanderson 1980).

But now we see something along the lines of the 'iron law of oligarchy' emerging. If the British approach to education in Sudan was flawed and likely to be counterproductive, this did not mean that the post-independence governments would behave any differently. Indeed, the new governments succeeded in taking over the various power structures over education imposed by the British, and in this lay the fruits of the civil war.

The Islamisation of the south that had begun before independence gained pace in 1956 as Britain handed over control to Khartoum. This movement to bring an Arabic and Islamic culture to the south has been seen positively and negatively: positively as a desire for a united Sudan and a way of trying to establish a national cultural identity, and negatively as a way of eliminating religious and cultural diversity (Deng 2006) and for the northern Sudanese to 'mould' the 'weak and underdeveloped' south along the Arab–Islamic lines of the north (Deng 2001). Bona Malwal (1981: 17) expresses the view that

> Many northern Sudanese had the notion that there were but a bunch of uncivilized tribes in the South, and very condescendingly, Northerners regarded themselves as guardians of these, their backward brethren.

Even if the goal had been to unite there is almost unanimous agreement that the result highlighted the differences and created division (Deng 2001):

> The North promoted Arabization and Islamization to establish national cultural unity, but their effect was in fact to widen the differences between the two parts of the country, escalating the conflict between them and giving it a racial and religious dimension that eventually reached genocidal proportions.

Much of the pressure towards Islam and an Arab identity came through the education system when, in 1957, the government nationalised all schools (ibid.), introduced Arabic as the language of instruction and infused the syllabus with Islamic concepts and Muslim teaching. The curriculum gave an Islamic point of view even in mathematics, physics and geography (Sommers 2005). Education was in decline and the 'Southerners had no say in curricular changes, which they viewed as imposed on them by a central system hostile to their culture and traditions' (Sommers 2005: 61, quoting UNICEF 2001).

An education system that had the potential to mitigate against division and to create a sense of shared identity was used to the opposite effect and became a means of increasing division (Breidlid 2010: 571):

> It was the Khartoum-based government's insistence on an ex- clusive narrative in the schools based on Arabic Islamism that necessitated, according to the southerners, an alternative nar- rative based on southern history and culture.

It is also recognised as a significant cause of the civil conflict, as education was either destroyed or 'bent to the [government's] needs' (Prendergast et al. 2002: 34). Deng (2006: 19):

> the education system during pre-war periods [between 1972 and 1982 in Sudan] contributed to the marginalization and ex- clusion of southern Sudanese and that largely contributed to the causation of the current civil war.

Sommers (2005: 19):

> Education for Southern Sudanese, where it has existed, has also been an enduring conflict issue: War has been fought, in part, over which curriculum and language of instruction should be used for educating Southern Sudanese.

Sommers (2005: 61):

> Narrowly available, mostly poor quality education and an im- posed language of instruction and curriculum have fuelled a succession of major conflicts in southern Sudan.

Although the mission schools were nationalised or closed and all missionaries forced to leave southern Sudan, alternative re- sources needed to improve and develop education in the south were not forthcoming from the government. At the same time the country plunged into violent conflict (beginning even before independence and developing into a full civil war by 1963), with the inevitable negative impact on education. Even during the inter-war period between 1972 and 1982 education resources were inadequate and well below the budget figures, leaving the system in a worse state relative to the north compared with the situation at independence (Table 25). For example, the primary school enrolment rate was about 40 per cent in the north but less than 12 per cent in the south (Deng 2006).

Table 25   Level of access to education in North and South Sudan during the inter-war period, 1972–83

Number of education facilities and population of students					
	North		South		Total
Primary pupils	1,349,000	90%	143,000	10%	1,492,000
Primary schools	5,343	87%	809	13%	6,152
Primary teachers	39,188	92%	3,432	8%	42,620
Gross enrolment ratio	40%		12%		
Pupil–teacher ratio	34		42		
Intermediate schools	1,378	93%	96	7%	1,474
Secondary schools	199	93%	15	7%	214
University admissions in 1983	3,499	99%	29	1%	3,528
Population percentage	72%		28%		100%

Sources: Deng (2006: 6, Table 2.2), using data from Yongo-Bure (1992).

Again it is clear that while the population proportion remains at 28 per cent, it is only the primary schools that reach above 10 per cent for the south, with a steady decline up through the education levels and only 1 per cent of the university population coming from the south. In 1976 it was estimated that over 90 per cent of the population of southern Sudan had never attended school (Sommers 2005). However, during the period of relative calm the successive central governments sought again to forge the Sudanese identity around the Arab–Islamic paradigm, with the education system becoming their means to implement this policy. These inequalities reignited the sense of injustice and exclusion that eventually led people in the south to resort again to armed struggle in 1982.

During the second period of civil conflict between 1983 and 2005 education again suffered, with the government unable to provide any education in rebel-held areas. In places where agencies were operating the emphasis was on humanitarian relief not education. At the time education was considered a part of 'development', which would only be expected to take hold after the end of the conflict. Peace must precede education, so 'the majority of international and bi-lateral donors were unwilling to support education in southern Sudan' (Brophy 2003: 9). Also, education was one of the underlying causes of the war and if an agency supported education in Arabic it could be perceived as supporting the government, while any that used another curriculum would be seen as opposing government policy (ibid.). Thus the way in which education had been so politicised meant that the educational efforts of the NGOs and agencies were hindered even in areas where the government held little or no sway.

Here we see how education made southern Sudanese society more prone to conflict through inadequate and unequal provision and through the imposition of values that increased social division. Had the British colonial government allowed greater educational provision through the missions then this would have reduced the sense of marginalisation and possibly allowed more southern Sudanese to progress into positions of influence and power. Their influence in Khartoum may have affected the decision-making processes and prevented divisive educational policies from being implemented. Also, had Arabic and the strong Islamic curriculum not been imposed, but rather the language and the manner of instruction been left to the people in the communities running the mission and other private schools, then education would probably not have been the focus of such antagonism towards the government. Overall it is clear that throughout the period under consideration, political decisions have been detrimental to the education and development of the people in South Sudan.

It seems that something like the 'iron law of oligarchy' was at play in Sudan. The colonial powers used education as a tool of oppression, and the post-colonial powers did more of the same. Therein lay the source of the conflict in South Sudan.

The iron law in Sierra Leone

In 1792, the British founded a colony on the Freetown peninsular for freed African-American slaves. The hinterland was included as a protectorate from 1896 and the two parts gained independence as a single country in 1961. The colony had a strong history of good Western education, boasting the first boy's grammar school (Sierra Leone Grammar School, founded 1845), the first girl's grammar school (Annie Walsh Memorial School, founded 1849), as well as the first tertiary education institution in sub-Saharan Africa (Fourah Bay College, founded 1827). This was affiliated with Durham University (World Bank 2007) and for 40 years provided training for Sierra Leoneans and other West Africans for the purpose of their employment in the colonial service (Banya 1993).

Education under the British began with the ex-slaves in the Freetown area (Banya 1993), but was later extended to the areas under indirect rule (the Protectorate), where it was limited to the 'ruling class' (Banya 1993). At independence, Sierra Leone inherited this British-type educational system that was largely academic, aimed at the urban middle class, and biased toward academically gifted students who entered tertiary education and found formal employment in government (World Bank 2007). Some argue it was perceived to be irrelevant to the needs of a rural population and left a majority of the population illiterate, never having been able to access even primary education (Novelli 2011: 9):

> British colonialism produced a highly elitist and geographically uneven education system, which was reproduced by post-colonial national elites after independence. Higher education and educational provision for elites was prioritized.

The very uneven geographic/social distribution of education in 1936 resulted in more than 50 per cent of the children in the colony of Freetown attending school compared with less than 3 per cent of those in the protectorate. By 1954, the percentage of children in school in the protectorate increased only to 8 per cent, while in Freetown approximately 85 per cent of children attended school. This meant that it was the Krio-speaking descendants of the freed slaves who were benefiting from the educational opportunities and access to jobs from the colonial period onwards (Novelli 2011).

Despite the geographic and gender inequality and emphasis on tertiary vis-à-vis primary education, the decision was made at independence to extend this system to all parts of the country (Banya 1991). So an academic education of an elitist nature, serving a minority and with a continuing emphasis on tertiary education (Banya 1993) and an ongoing discrepancy between the different regions remained after independence. Indeed, it has been suggested that (Banya 1993: 166):

> Independence further exacerbated the bias towards higher education as the urban middle and upper classes who had benefitted from the previous system became the political leaders. They and their cohorts benefitted heavily from the state-subsidised higher education. The education system thus continues to serve the poor badly and favour the urban over the rural areas.

Higher education and educational provision for the elites continued to be prioritised, with a high proportion of educational spending on higher education. This is despite policy documents that profess to prioritise basic education (Novelli 2011). In 1989 nearly 50 per cent of the education budget went on tertiary education, with only just over a quarter spent on secondary and elementary (Banya 1993). Even in the new millennium primary education received 24 per cent of the budget in 2009 and 25 per cent in 2010, against a benchmark of 50 per cent (Education for Change 2010).

The education system which began in British colonial times was continued and used to serve and perpetuate an elite who are generally urban (from the Western Area), middle or upper class and predominantly Krio or from the families of the ruling chiefs. Post-colonial governments 'tended to favour groups and regions which constitute their power base' (Wright 1997: 20).

As is the case for many conflicts, the causes of the civil war in Sierra Leone are complex and contested. There are of course competing claims that the conflict was either rooted in the greed of the political leaders or the genuine historical, structural and geographic grievances in the rest of society (Novelli 2011). However, whether the cause is one or the other (or a mixture of both), the role of education as a driver of Sierra Leone's conflict has been widely recognised (Fanthorpe 2003; Hanlon 2005; Boak and Dolan 2011; Ndaruhutse et al. 2011; Novelli 2011). This comes through in different ways.

Firstly, the youth combatants interviewed after the conflict are reported to have referred repeatedly to their lost educational opportunities and unmet aspirations before the conflict, citing them as a factor in their decision to fight (Peters and Richards 1998). One insightful militia fighter blamed the Revolutionary United Front (RUF) for the loss of home and educational prospects, but saw that their fighters were also frustrated students suffering because 'patrimonial politics sent a few to study to the highest level overseas and denied that opportunity to a majority, not on merit but on grounds of political favouritism' (ibid.: 187).

Secondly, the Revolutionary United Front (RUF), the main protagonist in the conflict, expressed its grievances regarding education in its 'Basic Document', signalling that the education system was incompatible with the needs and aspirations of the people of Sierra Leone. Moreover, the document clearly outlines something like the iron law of oligarchy, pointing out that the post-colonial government simply took over the methods of the colonial (Revolutionary United Front of Sierra Leone 1989):

> The educational system was initially a colonial imposition, which did not take into consideration the aspirations and needs of our people. The sole intention was to train passive and obedient Africans to man the colonial state structure. What was expected of any serious minded African ruling class was to radically alter the inherited educational system immediately after the attainment of independence. In our country, the ruling class simply continued from where the British colonialist left. Now it has become a common dictum of the APC ruling class that education is a privilege and not a right.

Education was already suffering not only through neglect but also through 'the corruption of government officials [which] helped to ensure ... a collapse in education' (Keen 2002/3). During the 1980s there was an economic crisis brought on, at least in part, by corruption and mismanagement (Zack-Williams 1999). Massive budget cuts were implemented as a consequence of the structural adjustment policies that were a condition of International Monetary Fund support during that decade (Novelli 2011). Education suffered: 'by 1986 education spending was one-sixth of what it had been five years before' (Hanlon 2005: 459) and according to Conteh-Morgan (2006: 99) suffered a budget cut of

50 per cent in 1987. All of this resulted in in teachers being unpaid, subsidies being removed and an increase in out-of-school youth on the streets. Industries were also closing down and unemployment reached 70 per cent, leaving the youth with little hope for the future (ibid.) and little access to the privileges of land and jobs that went through the patrimonial system run by the chiefs (Hanlon 2005; Humphreys and Weinstein 2008). Joining the militia was seen as the best alternative (Peters and Richards 1998: 183):

> ... many under-age combatants choose to fight with their eyes open, and defend their choice, sometimes proudly. Set against a background of destroyed families and failed educational systems, militia activity offers young people a chance to make their way in the world.

The RUF sought to capitalise on this 'socially excluded youth underclass' and recruited extensively from 'the swollen ranks of educational drop-outs' (Peters and Richards 1998: 184, 187). The situation where the elite were benefiting themselves and controlling others through a corrupt educational system became worse as education, along with health, police and the military, further collapsed and the civil conflict started. As the war progressed the government's capacity to provide education was eroded, particularly in the rural areas where it was almost entirely halted (Novelli 2011). Around 70 per cent of the children in the country were left with no access to education towards the end of the conflict (Sharkey 2008).

Thirdly, not only did the lack of education fuel grievances and act as a push factor towards militancy and civil war, but also the rhetoric of the RUF, with its emphasis on education, inclusion and change, encouraged hopes of a better future when the corrupt regime would be replaced (Humphreys and Weinstein 2008: 441 (emphasis added)):

Rebels and civilians alike saw the rebellion as a chance to *resume their education* and to express their discontent with the misuse of Sierra Leone's diamond wealth for politicians' personal gain.

The way in which the 'iron law' appeared to work in Sierra Leone can be summed up in the observations of the Truth and Reconciliation Commission (2004):

> Successive regimes became increasingly impervious to the wishes and needs of the majority. Instead of implementing positive and progressive policies, each regime perpetuated the ills and self-serving machinations left behind by its predecessor.

In these ways government education policy and action can be seen to have been major contributors to the civil confict in Sierra Leone between 1991 and 2002.

The iron law in Liberia

The iron law usefully characterises what happened in both South Sudan and Sierra Leone. Their histories illustrate how education and conflict are interwoven, under colonial rule and then after independence. The case of Liberia is similar – although perhaps even more remarkable. Liberia is often described as a country which was not colonised. This is not strictly true. Indeed, the history of Liberia is perhaps one of the most extraordinary on the continent. Freed slaves from America arrived and created in effect their own colony – complete with their own slaves – ruling over the indigenous Africans.

Liberia, literally 'land of the free', was founded in 1822 as a colony for former slaves. Thousands of freed slaves and free-born African-Americans soon settled in the country, despite the presence of indigenous communities, many of which were opposed to these new colonists. The settler minority then took the political lead to establish the country as an independent nation in 1847. This early American-born leadership formed an elite group and perpetuated a double-tiered social structure in which local African peoples could not achieve full participation in the nation's social, civic and political life. The dualistic system functioned because the Americo-Liberians, as the settlers were called, established exclusive political, economic and social institutions, and used these institutions to promote their own interests and maintain their dominance (Inter-Agency Network for Education in Emergencies 2011).

Shortly after the establishment of Liberia as an independent nation in 1847 the Americo-Liberians passed a law that prohibited the education of any indigenous people, apparently in an effort to control the 95 per cent of the population that formed the African-Liberians, as the indigenous population was called. Through lack of education and disenfranchisement the Americo-Liberians operated a slave-master system in Liberia, perpetuating the same harsh and unjust treatment on the African-Liberians as they themselves had suffered as former slaves in the US (Dillon 2008).

Thus most of the infrastructure and basic services, including formal education, were concentrated in Monrovia and the few other cities where most of the Americo-Liberians lived. Government-provided education failed to reach the indigenous rural population. Formal schooling was particularly geared to educating the Americo-Liberian society, with only 'bush' schools serving the indigenous population. These indigenous schools ('Poro' for boys and 'Sande' for girls) played an important role in providing basic education and training, including discipline and the communication of indigenous culture (Lanier 1961), but were not able to bridge the educational gap between the indigenous people and the urban settlers.

Despite the efforts and policies of 'unification', 'open door', and 'integration', particularly by President William Tubman after World War II, aiming for a more inclusive society, this divide has remained. And political, economic and social marginalisation and exclusion were at the core of grievances that led to civil conflict (Inter-Agency Network for Education in Emergencies 2011). The Truth and Reconciliation Commission (2009: 16) indicated that one of the key causes of the conflict was the

> Entrenched political and social system founded on privilege, patronage, politicization of the military and endemic corruption which created limited access to education and justice, economic and social opportunities and amenities.

Not only is this the considered judgement of those entrusted with the task of explaining 'how Liberia became what it is today' (ibid.), but it is also the shared experience of ordinary Liberians, as reported by the INEE (2011: 32) in its research:

> ... several interviewees spoke of the connections they saw between education and conflict, as well as of the importance of education for their children, for the nation, and for the sake of peace.

Another interviewee commented on the divisions and patronage in education and society (ibid.: 33):

> The indigenous people were deprived of high level positions. In the entire history of Liberia to 1980, only one indigenous person was a minister of foreign affairs. None minister of internal affairs, none speaker of the house, and none head of the senate. So all these factors [contributed to the war]. Before the fighting, the education standard was very low. The University of Liberia never had graduate studies. Because the descendants of the elite went to America. They were only here for high school. They went abroad on government scholarships. So the system reproduced itself.

Education was established in a double-tiered and elitist manner, supporting the extractive structures in society. It was this effort to maintain the privileges of the Americo-Liberians which, according to Dillon's analysis, led to their own downfall and the destruction of the country (2008).

If inequality and exclusion were drivers for conflict, it might be expected that the coup in 1980 by Samuel Kanyon Doe, which brought the first African-Liberian to power and was considered an act to reverse Americo-Liberian's domination of political and economic power, would result in a change to the culture (and education) in the country. However, this was not to be: the coup just transferred power and privilege from one ethnic group to another (Williams 2004) and thus perpetuated the social and economic inequalities. This is a further example of the 'iron law of oligarchy', where a revolution replaces one tyranny with another, with 'new leaders overthrowing old ones with promises of radical change', but bringing 'nothing but more of the same' (Acemoglu and Robinson 2013: 361).

Conclusion

A new approach to the role of private schools in conflict-affected states puts them at the forefront of educational delivery. Evidence shows there are educational entrepreneurs, working in both profit and non-profit sectors, who are able and willing to take on educational responsibilities – and they do it much better than government. Low-cost private schools should be seen as playing a fundamental role in development in these countries, not as a temporary expedient.

Such an approach could bring considerable advantages. The potential for corruption in the state could be reduced if its role in education were scaled back. And the private sector, with its higher academic standards, would be more effective at creating an educated populace, a bulwark against an oppressive state.

Most significantly, in each of the states surveyed, government education policy has clearly been used as a tool of oppression of the people, initially by colonial governments, but then by post-colonial governments too, following the 'iron law of oligarchy'. The history of educational provision in South Sudan, Sierra Leone and Liberia in each case reveals to an extraordinary extent how governments have used education to repress and control the people, and how government education policies have been a root cause of conflict. Those in positions of power controlled and manipulated the education of generations of young people for their own ends and to achieve their political goals.

Unfortunately, there is always a danger, particularly in failed states, that those in power may again resort to patronage or oppression. Indeed the OECD reports that education appears to be one of the services most prone to 'polarisation and manipulation' (OECD 2008: 9). If the government's power over education can be reduced, then the potential to use it for harm can also be significantly reduced.

The danger of allowing governments control over education in fragile states is clear, as education is a very ready tool for oppression. Removing education as far as possible from the power of states could therefore help fragile states avoid getting sucked back into a vicious cycle of oppression leading to violence.

6 CONCLUSIONS: REDUCING THE POWER OF THE STATE IN EDUCATION

Low-cost private schools are ubiquitous across the developing world. In previous research we have catalogued their nature and extent in a range of countries including Ghana, Nigeria, Kenya, India and China. For this book, we embarked on another journey to see if they were also present in conflict-affected states in sub-Saharan Africa. Certainly, the accepted wisdom, which we dubbed the standard approach to education in conflict-affected states, seems to accept that at least some kind of fee-paying schools emerge during conflict. However, the same accepted wisdom says that these private schools should be tolerated only as a temporary expedient: what is required in fragile states is the same as in any other state, a strong Ministry of Education running schools for all.

Harnessing evidence from our recent research in South Sudan, Sierra Leone and Liberia, we both agreed with, and challenged, the standard approach. Certainly, parental demand led to fee-paying schools emerging, but these were of many types. They included proprietor or for-profit schools, not just 'community' schools (which seemed to be an implication of the standard approach). Crucially, private schools, especially for-profit schools, tended to emerge in largest numbers *after* the conflict was over. Moreover, these private schools had many advantages over government schools – typically, they showed higher academic performance and were much better value for money. They were also affordable to the poor and were not biased against girls.

Clearly, not every child is in private school – but certainly a majority are in the urban, peri-urban and rural areas surveyed, with a significant minority likely in other rural areas. Given that governments in fragile states already have a hard enough job in addressing urgent needs such as security, the rule of law and implementing democracy, it seemed odd that international agencies were trying to get them to accomplish yet more – by taking over a functioning and still growing private sector. This could be characterised as 'pre-mature load bearing' (see Pritchett et al. 2010).

Instead of the standard approach, we suggest an altogether different way of addressing education in conflict-affected states. Our new approach is to embrace the private sector in education, recognising its ubiquity, its superiority over government schools, and its positive social impact. Rather than seeing the burgeoning fee-paying schools as a temporary expedient, our approach says we should embrace them as desirable providers of educational provision, including for the poor. This is the central argument of this book.

Reducing the role of government in education appeared to have many advantages too – and here again we agreed with the first proposition of the standard approach, which suggests that government education policy itself is often a significant contributing factor to conflict. Exploring the dramatic history of the three countries researched showed that government policies and actions in education were indeed major factors in the conflicts that emerged. Taking away as far as possible the temptation – and the possibility – for governments of fragile states to use education for their own ends seemed a very positive outcome.

Moving education as far as possible outside of government control could also be a positive way of reducing corruption. And because private schooling delivers superior quality to government schooling, allowing education to be as much as possible outside of government could also deliver a better-educated populace, potentially a bulwark against the risk of government oppression.

Notice that the approach we are proposing may not be privatisation as normally understood. This is a process whereby government assigns businesses or services to private rather than state control or ownership. This generally features a top-down approach: for example, governments 'denationalise' particular industries. What we are describing here is something a bit different, for there is already a 'bottom-up' or 'grassroots' privatisation, where the people themselves, not the state, are engaged in re-assigning education to private rather than state control and ownership. Governments should go with the grain of that grassroots revolution.

What policy implications do these conclusions bring? Currently, when working in fragile, conflict-affected states, international and donor agencies such as the UK's Department for International Development (DFID) are focused on creating, improving and expanding the remit of ministries of education (as well as other ministries) as their way of improving education. Our alternative policy proposal suggests that this is neither sensible nor efficient if the goal is to improve educational outcomes and opportunity. Government ministries of education do of course have to look after existing government educational provision. But a major underlying aim of any international involvement should be to increasingly move educational provision away from government. Every effort should be taken to ensure that any initiative takes the potential for private delivery into account.

Governments are typically involved in education in three ways, through regulation, funding and provision. How could these three areas change under our proposed programme?

Regulation

Government regulation can be very harmful to low-cost private education, serving to damage educational opportunities for the poorest. This has become clear in India, for instance, where the

Right to Education Act (RTE) has focused on inputs, insisting low-cost private schools have the same level of inputs as higher-cost schools, thus undermining their financial viability. This has led to the closure of many thousands of low-cost private schools (see, for example, Francis 2014). Thus parents are being forced to send their children back to government schools which they rejected in favour of the private schools being forced to close, even though research supports parents' preferences, showing that low-cost private schools have superior academic performance to government schools (Tooley 2016).

There are better kinds of regulation which can serve to enable private education rather than stifle it. A first step for any donor agency involved in education in conflict-affected states must be to help governments create unobtrusive and enabling regulations for the private education sector, allowing it to flourish and continue to serve poor communities.

The work of DFID, through its organisation DEEPEN, in the regulation of private education in Lagos State, Nigeria, may be a useful model in this regard. DEEPEN is working closely with the government and federations of private schools, especially AFED – the Association of Formidable Educational Development, an association with around 5,000 low-cost private schools as members.[1] One of its work-streams is the 'Graded Assessment of Private Schools' (GAPS) programme, which aims to grade schools based on how they are working towards improving standards, judged against research-based criteria of how school improvement works.

The key policy point is that regulatory environments for private education should be explored and assessed in terms of how they allow the private sector to flourish and provide better quality educational provision. Any regulations that do not do this should be avoided.

---

1   Disclosure: Tooley is the international patron of AFED.

A second step also suggests itself. The discussion in Chapter 5 suggests that regulations concerning the curriculum can be the source of conflict. The policy suggestion is that they therefore should be avoided as far as possible. The problems of conflict-affected states have often been the explicit result of previous governments dictating the curriculum to the detriment of already disadvantaged or oppressed groups. Policy-makers and their international funders should try to avoid the temptation to get involved in this fraught area. Indeed, given the historical origins of some of the curricula imposed on rural communities, perhaps designed to oppress rather than to liberate, it may be that international partners can explore ways of making the curriculum more appropriate and less exploitative. However, the temptation should be avoided to make any curricula arising out of such initiatives compulsory. Instead, incentives could be offered to private sector providers to market-test new curricula and, if appropriate, roll them out as private sector initiatives, open to competition rather than set in stone as government monopoly regulation.

Funding

The examples of how low-cost private schools are serving poor communities suggest that education is something that parents are willing and, in many cases, able to pay for. So in many cases, funding of education may not be required.

What about those areas where there are lower levels of private-sector provision, such as rural areas distant from capital cities? And, if the aim is to reduce the role of government in education as much as possible, what about those children not in private schools in areas where private provision is in the majority?

Here, there are many possibilities for targeted funding. One possibility is through targeted vouchers or scholarships, to be given to the most vulnerable groups or those not currently served well by private education (for example, in remote rural areas). This not only allows them to access private education, but also lets educational entrepreneurs see market possibilities in areas which may otherwise be too poor to make entry feasible (see Tooley 2009; West 1994). Such funding could come through governments or international agencies. There are examples of this happening with relative success in Pakistan (see Day Ashley et al. 2014), and such examples could be copied elsewhere. The key here is as far as possible not to supplant parental involvement in their children's education and the accountability that emerges through parents paying fees, but to supplement it where, for example, genuine hardship prevents access to private schools.

Importantly, funding should go only to the families, to help supplement their income, not to schools. It is not up to ministries or outsiders to decide which schools are deserving of funding, only to help parents make those decisions where they have difficulty paying fees. (The example of government assistance to private schools in Sierra Leone is informative in this regard, as discussed earlier).

Another possibility is emerging, at the time of writing, in Liberia. The government of Liberia has contracted out around 100 of its schools to private sector companies, with support from international philanthropy organisations (see Mungai 2016). This includes chains of low-cost private schools such as Bridge International Academies, BRAC, Rising Academies and Omega Schools Franchise Ltd.[2] Importantly, this is seen as a pilot and eventually it may be that *all* of the government's schools are contracted out in this way.

This certainly seems like an effective way of quickly reaching remote rural populations (many of the schools to be contracted out are in such areas). If so, it could potentially very speedily bring in better quality providers with a track record of achievement.

2   Disclosure: Tooley is chairman and co-founder of Omega Schools.

However, the approach may have some drawbacks, which in the medium and long term may make it less effective than targeted vouchers or scholarships, as outlined above.

Firstly, the teachers in the government schools will remain civil servants. This means that the size of the public sector will not diminish if this is the main approach to education reform, and the advantages of a reduced role for government in education may not emerge. Moreover, the teachers will not be accountable to the private companies involved, suggesting that there may be an uphill struggle to improve educational quality. Teacher accountability has been identified as a possible major reason why private schools are successful (Tooley 2009).

Secondly, the approach may serve to harm some indigenous educational entrepreneurs who are already serving the poor. Instead of funding outside education companies to take over government schools, it may be preferable to find equivalent funding so that existing private school providers could flourish where they are already present, or could seek to expand into areas in which market penetration is low (for example, remote rural areas). Again, a good method could be to provide full or partial scholarships to those in hardship or in underserved areas, allowing private schools to compete for this additional income stream through parental choice.

Provision

The methods suggested above are likely, in the medium and long term, to reduce the amount of required public provision of education, i.e. government schools. The argument of this book is that there is little or no need for governments in fragile states to be concerned with providing education. Certainly, there is no need for such governments to *increase* their provision of schools. If there are areas of increasing demand for education, then it is likely that the private sector will step in to meet that demand, or will do so if provided with the kinds of targeted funding high-lighted above.

Outside these three areas, the key to 'going with the grain' of private sector involvement in education is knowledge and un-derstanding of the nature and extent of that sector. An impor-tant area in which international agencies can get involved is in research and dissemination: find out as much as possible about the current nature and extent of private education provision, especially for the poor, and especially in more remote rural and smaller urban areas. We have set out the research we conducted along these lines in three conflict-affected states, but we were only able to examine what was going on in the capital cities and their environs. More research is needed: not research for research's sake, but research to inform the minimal policy that we have recommended. So, commission research and then dis-seminate it widely, to explore the role that private education can play in development.

Situations of conflict and fragility bring out the worst and best in people. They challenge and destroy lives, infrastructure and livelihoods. They can be the culmination of years of low devel-opment and exploitation or may signal the beginning of further human suffering. However, the end of conflict is an opportun-ity for change, a critical juncture in the life of a community or a nation, the chance for a new direction as old power structures and hierarchies are weakened or dismantled and new structures emerge or are deliberately embraced.

Education is one area where freedom needs to be extended, and it is one where freedom is relatively easy to allow, because the conflict itself often opens the door for that freedom. We have seen that in conflict-affected states people have responded to the de-struction of government schools by creating new, more extensive and inclusive educational opportunities. This open door must not be closed.

The system of government-provided education that is being advocated by international agencies has been shown not to be particularly effective in more capable and less fragile countries such as Nigeria or India. There is even less capacity to achieve positive results in fragile, conflict-affected states. However, given that there is already a system emerging with dedicated practitioners and an enthusiastic clientele, it would be foolish to limit, hinder or deny its growth or expansion. Such private endeavours must be nurtured, not stifled, so that these schools can grow into an effective, culturally appropriate and accountable system, serving their local communities and the nation.

REFERENCES

Acemoglu, D. and Robinson, J. A. (2013) *Why Nations Fail: The Origins of Power, Prosperity and Poverty.* London: Profile Books.

All Africa (2014) Liberia: 15 of 13,000 Successfully Pass Univ. of Liberia Entrance Exams. Front Page Africa. Available at http://allafrica.com/stories/201410221209.html (accessed 22 March 2016).

Andrabi, T., Das, J. and Khwaja, A. (2008) A dime a day: the possibilities and limits of private schooling in Pakistan. *Comparative Education Review* 52(3): 329–55.

Banya, K. (1991) Economic decline and the education system: the case of Sierra Leone. *Compare: A Journal of Comparative and International Education* 21(2): 127–43.

Banya, K. (1993) Illiteracy, colonial legacy and education: the case of modern Sierra Leone. *Comparative Education* 29(2): 159–70.

Batley, R. and Mcloughlin, C. (2010) Engagement with non-state service providers in fragile states: reconciling state-building and service delivery. *Development Policy Review* 28(2): 131–54.

BBC News (2013) Liberia students all fail university admission exam. 26 August. Available at: http://www.bbc.co.uk/news/world-africa-23843578 (accessed 22 March 2016).

Boak, E. and Dolan, J. (2011) *State-building, Peace-building and Service Delivery in Fragile and Conflict-affected States. Case Study: Sierra Leone.* Reading: CfBT.

Bold, T., Kimenyi, M., Mwabu, G. and Sandefur, J. (2013) *The High Return to Private Schooling in a Low-Income Country.* Washington, DC: Brookings.

Breidlid, A. (2010) Sudanese images of the other: education and conflict in Sudan. *Comparative Education Review* 54(4): 555–75.

Brophy, M. (2003) *Progress to Universal Primary Education in Southern Sudan: A Short Country Case Study.* Paris: UNESCO.

Brown, G. (2012) *Education in South Sudan: Investing in a Better Future.* London: The Office of Gordon and Sarah Brown.

Buckland, P. (2006) Post-conflict education: time for a reality check? *Forced Migration Review* 26 (supplement): 7–8.

Collins, R. O. (1983) *Shadows in the Grass: Britain in the Southern Sudan, 1918–1956.* New Haven and London: Yale University Press.

Conteh-Morgan, E. (2006) Globalization, state failure and collective violence: the case of Sierra Leone. *International Journal of Peace Studies* 11(2): 87–104.

Day Ashley, L., Mcloughlin, C., Aslam, M., Engel, J., Wales, J., Rawal, S., Batley, R., Kingdon, G., Nicolai, S. and Rose, P. (2014) *The Role and Impact of Private Schools in Developing Countries: A Rigorous Review of the Evidence. Final Report.* London: IPPI Centre.

Deng, F. M. (1995) *War of Visions: Conflict of Identities in the Sudan.* Washington, DC: Brookings Institution.

Deng, F. M. (2001) Sudan – civil war and genocide: disappearing Christians of the Middle East. *Middle East Quarterly* 8(1): 13–21. Available at http://www.meforum.org/22/sudan-civil-war-and-genocide

Deng, L. B. (2006) Education in Southern Sudan: war, status and challenges of achieving education for all goals. *Respect, Sudanese Journal for Human Rights' Culture and Issues of Cultural Diversity* 4: 1–27.

Dillon, E. C. (2008) The role of education in the rise and fall of Americo-Liberians in Liberia, West Africa (1980). Dissertation, Georgia State University.

Economist (2015) The $1-a-week school. *The Economist* 416(8949): 7.

Education for Change (2010) *Design and Development of a Comprehensive Education Sector Capacity Development Strategy.* London. Available at www.efc.co.uk

Express Tribune (2012) Education corruption: 'illegal' appointments challenged in Sindh High Court (accessed 25 November 2015).

Fanthorpe, R. (2003) Humanitarian aid in post-war Sierra Leone: the politics of moral economy. In *Power, Livelihoods and Conflict: Case*

Studies in Political Economy Analysis for Humanitarian Action (ed. S. Collinson). London: Overseas Development Institute.

Francis, A. (2014) Why India's landmark education law is shutting down schools. BBC News, 6 March. Available at http://www.bbc.com/news/world-asia-india-26333713 (accessed 2 April 2016).

Fund for Peace (2015) *Fragile States Index, 2015*. 24 November 2015. Washington, DC: The Fund for Peace. Available at http://fsi.fundfor peace.org/

Ghani, A. and Lockhart, C. (2008) *Fixing Failed States, a Framework for Rebuilding a Fractured World*. New York: Oxford University Press.

Goldsmith, C. (2010) 'Teachers' pay – making the pipe work': the role of improving teachers' payroll systems for education service delivery and state legitimacy in selected conflict-affected countries in Africa. Background paper prepared for the Education for All Global Monitoring Report 2011. Paris: UNESCO.

Gove, A. and Wetterberg, A. (2011) *The Early Grade Reading Assessment: Applications and Interventions to Improve Basic Literacy*. Research Triangle Park, NC: RTI International.

Government of Liberia (2011) *A New Education Reform Act 2011*. Monrovia: Government of Liberia.

Government of Sierra Leone (1991) *The Constitution of Sierra Leone, 1991*. Available at http://www.sierra-leone.org/Laws/constitution1991.pdf.

Government of Sierra Leone (2004) *The Education Act, 2004*. Freetown: Sierra Leone Gazette. Available at http://www.sierra-leone.org/Laws/2004–2p.pdf

Government of Sierra Leone (2010) *Millennium Development Goals Progress Report 2010*. Freetown.

Government of South Sudan (2011) *Educational Statistics for Central Equatoria*. Juba.

Hanlon, J. (2005) Is the international community helping to recreate the preconditions for war in Sierra Leone? *The Round Table* 94(381): 459–72.

Health and Education Advice and Resource Team (2012) *DFID South Sudan Education Programme, Construction & Rehabilitation of Edu-*

cation Facilities – Construction Review. Available at http://www.heart
-resources.org/assignment/dfid-south-sudan-education-progra
mme-construction-rehabilitation-of-education-facilities/ (accessed
12 October 2015).

Humphreys, M. and Weinstein, J. M. (2008) Who fights? The determi-
nants of participation in civil war. *American Journal of Political Science* 52(2): 436–55.

Inter-Agency Network for Education in Emergencies (2010) *Minimum
Standards for Education: Preparedness, Response, Recovery*. New
York: INEE [Online]. Available at: http://toolkit.ineesite.org/toolkit/
INEEcms/uploads/1012/INEE_GuideBook_EN_2012%20LoRes.pdf

Johnson, D. H. (2003) *The Root Causes of Sudan's Civil Wars*. Oxford and
Indiana: The International Africa Institute/Indiana University Press.

Keen, D. (2002/3) Conflict, trade and economic agendas. *Committee for
Conflict Transformation Support Newsletter* 19.

Khatete, I. and Asiago, D. (2013) Effectiveness of the board of governors
in the recruitment of secondary school teachers in Gucha District.
Journal of Education and Practice 4(28): 63–68.

Lanier, R. O. H. (1961) The problem of mass education in Liberia. *The
Journal of Negro Education* 30(3): 251–60.

Leh Di Pipul Tok (2006) *Report on Basic Education in Sierra Leone*. Freetown: Campaign for Good Governance. Available at www.slcgg.org.

Lewin, K. M. (2007) *The Limits to Growth of Non-Government: Private
Schooling in Sub Saharan Africa*. Project Report. Falmer, UK: Con-
sortium for Research on Educational Access, Transitions and Equity
(CREATE).

Longfield, D. (2015a) Education in post-conflict zones: a case study of
South Sudan. In *Handbook of International Development and Education* (ed. P. Dixon, S. Humble and C. Counihan), pp. 232–48. Chelten-
ham: Edward Elgar Publishing.

Longfield, D. (2015b) Educational development in South Sudan: con-
scious design or spontaneous order? *Economic Affairs* 35(2): 178–96.

Longfield, D. and Tooley, J. (2013) *A Survey of Schools in Juba, South Sudan*.
Newcastle: E. G. West Centre. Available at http://egwestcentre.files

.wordpress.com/2014/07/00-report-south-sudan-2013–11–30.pdf (accessed 25 March 2015).

Malwal, B. (1981) *People and Power in Sudan – The Struggle for National Stability*. London: Ithaca Press.

Ministry of Education (2010) *The Education Sector Plan of Liberia – A Commitment to Making a Difference*. Monrovia.

Ministry of Education (2011) *Liberian Education Administrative Regulations*. Monrovia.

Ministry of Education, Science and Technology (2007) *Sierra Leone Education Sector Plan: A Road Map to a Better Future 2007–2015*. Freetown: MEST.

Ministry of Education Science and Technology (2012) *Making Progress – Schools and Students in Sierra Leone. The 2010/11 School Census Report*. Freetown.

Ministry of Planning and Economic Affairs/UNDP (2010) *Republic of Liberia: Progress, Prospects and Challenges towards Achieving the MDGs*. Monrovia.

Mungai, C. (2016) An Africa first! Liberia outsources entire education system to a private American firm. Why all should pay attention. *Mail and Guardian Africa*, 31 March. Available at http://mgafrica.com/article/2016–03–31-liberia-plans-to-outsource-its-entire-education-system-to-a-private-company-why-this-is-a-very-big-deal-and-africa-should-pay-attention.

Ndaruhutse, S., Ali, M., Chandran, R., Cleaver, F., Dolan, J., Sondorp, E. and Vaux, T. (2011) *State-Building, Peace-Building and Service Delivery in Fragile and Conflict-Affected States: Literature Review*. London: DfID.

Novelli, M. (2011) *The Role of Education in Peacebuilding: Case Study – Sierra Leone*. New York: United Nations Children's Fund.

O'Neill, R. (2014) Perpetuating a vicious cycle: the causes and effects of poorly educated children in Sierra Leone. *Global Majority E-Journal* 5(1): 44–56.

Oduho, J. and Deng, W. (1963) *The Problem of the Southern Sudan*. London: Oxford University Press.

OECD (2008) *Service Delivery in Fragile Situations: Key Concepts, Findings and Lessons.* Paris: Organisation for Economic Co-operation and Development.

Peah, C. T. L. (2013) Liberia 2013–2014 Draft National Budget Analysis Public Sector Investment Plan (PSIP). Monrovia, Liberia Institute of Public Opinion.

Peters, K. and Richards, P. (1998) 'Why we fight': voices of youth combatants in Sierra Leone. *Africa: Journal of the International African Institute* 68(2): 183–210.

Pôle de Dakar (2013) *Education Country Status Report Sierra Leone: An Analysis for Further Improving the Quality, Equity and Efficiency of the Education System in Sierra Leone.* Dakar: UNESCO.

Poverty Reduction Economic Management Sector Unit (PREM 4) (2009) Liberia 2008 Public Expenditure Management and Financial Accountability Review. Africa Development Bank/World Bank.

Prendergast, J., Galic, M., Dubey, R., Roessler, P. and Macgregor, D. (2002) *God, Oil and Country: Changing the Logic of War in Sudan.* Brussels: International Crisis Group.

Pritchett, L., Woolcock, M. and Andrews, M. (2010) *Capability Traps? The Mechanisms of Persistent Implementation Failure.* Working Paper 234. Washington, DC: Center for Global Development. Available at http://www.cgdev.org/files/1424651_file_Pritchett_Capability_FINAL.pdf.

Republic of South Sudan (2012) *General Education Strategic Plan, 2012 – 2017: Promoting Learning for All* (Draft). Juba: Ministry of General Education and Instruction. Available at http://planipolis.iiep .unesco.org/upload/South%20Sudan/South_Sudan_General_Education_Plan_2012_2017.pdf.

Revolutionary United Front of Sierra Leone (1989) *Basic Document of the Revolutionary United Front of Sierra Leone: The Second Liberation of Africa.* Available at www.fas.org/irp/world/para/docs/footpaths. htm.

Sanderson, L. P. (1980) Education in the Southern Sudan: the impact of government-missionary-Southern Sudanese relationships upon the development of education during the Condominium Period, 1898–1956. *African Affairs* 79(315): 157–69.

Sharkey, D. (2008) Contradictions in girls' education in a post-conflict setting. *Compare: A Journal of Comparative and International Education* 38(5): 569–79.

Singh, K. (2015) *Protecting the Right to Education against Commercialization* (A/HRC/29/30). New York: United Nations Special Rapporteur on the right to education. Available at http://www.right-to-education.org/sites/right-to-education.org/files/resource-attachments/UNSR_Report_HRC_Commercialisation_Education_2015.pdf

Sommers, M. (2005) *Islands of Education: Schooling, Civil War and the Southern Sudanese (1983–2004).* Paris: International Institute for Educational Planning (IIEP) UNESCO.

Sudan Tribune (2014) S. Sudan finance minister tables $4 billion budget before parliament. Available at http://sudantribune.com/spip.php?article51551 (accessed 29 October 2015).

Swazi Observer (2015) Teachers allege rot, bribery, extortion at education. Available at http://www.observer.org.sz/news/75374-teachers-allege-rot-bribery-extortion-at-education.html (accessed 25 November 2015).

Tooley, J. (2009) *The Beautiful Tree: A Personal Journey into How the World's Poorest People Are Educating Themselves.* New Delhi: Penguin.

Tooley, J. (2012) Big questions and poor economics: Banerjee and Duflo on schooling in developing countries. *Econ Journal Watch* 9(3): 170–85.

Tooley, J. (2013) Challenging educational injustices: 'grassroots' privatisation in South Asia and Sub-Saharan Africa. Special Issue of *Oxford Review of Education* on 'Privatisation of Education and Social Justice' (ed. G. Walford).

Tooley, J. (2015) Low cost private schools: controversies and implications concerning EFA debate. *ZEP (Zeitschrift für Internationale Bildungsforschung und Entwicklungspädagogik)* 38(2): 22–27.

Tooley, J. (2016) Extending access to low-cost private schools through vouchers: an alternative interpretation of a two-stage 'school choice' experiment in India. *Oxford Review of Education* 42(5): 579–93.

Tooley, J., Dixon, P. and Stanfield, J. (2008) Impact of free primary education in Kenya: a case study of private schools in Kibera. *Educational Management Administration and Leadership* 36(4): 449–69.

Tooley, J. and Longfield, D. (2014a) *Private Education in Low-Income Areas of Monrovia: School and Household Surveys.* Newcastle: E. G. West Centre and Development Initiatives Liberia, I.

Tooley, J. and Longfield, D. (2014b) *Private Primary Education in Western Area, Sierra Leone.* Newcastle: E. G. West Centre Newcastle University and Peoples' Education Association.

Tooley, J. and Longfield, D. (2015) *The Role and Impact of Low-Cost Private Schools in Developing Countries: A Response to the DFID-Commissioned Rigorous Literature Review.* London: Pearson.

Tooley, J. and Longfield, D. (2016) Affordability of private schools: exploration of a conundrum and towards a definition of 'low-cost'. *Oxford Review of Education* 42(4): 444–59.

Transparency International (2015) *Corruption Perceptions Index 2014: Results.* 25 November. Berlin: Transparency International. Available at http://www.transparency.org/cpi2014/results.

Truth and Reconciliation Commission (2004) *Final Report of the Truth and Reconciliation Commission of Sierra Leone.* Freetown. Available at http://www.sierra-leone.org/Other-Conflict/TRCVolume1.pdf.

Truth and Reconciliation Commission of Liberia (2009) *Consolidated Final Report*, Volume II. Monrovia: Government of Liberia.

UNESCO (2000) *The Dakar Framework for Action: Education for All – Meeting our Collective Commitments (Including Six Regional Frameworks for Action)* (Adopted by the World Education Forum, Dakar, 26–28 April). Paris: UNESCO.

UNESCO (2003) *Education in Situations of Emergency, Crisis and Reconstruction.* ED-2003/WS/48. Paris: UNESCO Strategy.

UNESCO (2011) *EFA Global Monitoring Report. The Hidden Crisis: Armed Conflict and Education.* Paris: UNESCO.

UNESCO/IIEP (2010) *Guidebook for Planning Education in Emergencies and Reconstruction.* Paris: International Institute for Educational Planning.

UNICEF (2001) *Education for All: Assessment Report Southern Sudan 2001*. Nairobi: UNICEF.

UNICEF (2012) Liberia country study: profiles of children out of school. Global initiative on out-of-school children. UNICEF and UNESCO Institute of Statistics.

Watkins, K. (2012) Basic services in South Sudan. In *One Year after Independence, Opportunities and Obstacles for Africa's Newest Country*. Washington, DC: Brookings Institution.

Watkins, K. (2013) *Accelerating Progress to 2015 South Sudan*. Washington, DC: Brookings Institution.

West, E. G. (1994) *Education and the State: A Study in Political Economy*, 3rd edn (1st edn, 1965). Indianapolis: Liberty Fund.

Williams, A. M. (2004) The Liberian saga: one nation, two cultures. The perspective. Monrovia: Liberian democratic future. http://www.the perspective.org/saga.html

World Bank (2005) *Reshaping the Future: Education and Post-Conflict Reconstruction*. Washington, DC: World Bank.

World Bank (2007) *Education in Sierra Leone: Present Challenges, Future Opportunities*. Washington. DC: World Bank.

World Bank (2010) Out of the ashes – learning lessons from the past to guide education recovery in Liberia. Liberia Education Country Status Report, Washington.

World Bank (2013) Multi-donor trust fund for South Sudan: improving life for South Sudan's 8.3 million people. Available at http://www .worldbank.org/en/news/feature/2013/05/28/multi-donor-trust -fund-for-south-sudan-improving-life-for-south-sudan-s-8–3-mil lion-people (accessed 29 October 2015).

World Education Forum (2000) *Education in Situations of Emergency and Crisis: Challenges for the New Century*. Dakar: UNESCO.

Wright, C. (1997) *Educational Destruction and Reconstruction in Disrupted Societies*. Geneva: International Bureau of Education/University of Geneva

Yongo-Bure, B. (1992) The underdevelopment of the Southern Sudan since independence. In *Civil War in the Sudan* (ed. M. Daly and A. Sikainga). London: British Academic Press.

Zack-Williams, A. B. (1999) Sierra Leone: the political economy of civil war, 1991–98. *Third World Quarterly* 20(1): 143–62.

ABOUT THE IEA

The Institute is a research and educational charity (No. CC 235 351), limited by guarantee. Its mission is to improve understanding of the fundamental institutions of a free society by analysing and expounding the role of markets in solving economic and social problems.

The IEA achieves its mission by:

- a high-quality publishing programme
- conferences, seminars, lectures and other events
- outreach to school and college students
- brokering media introductions and appearances

The IEA, which was established in 1955 by the late Sir Antony Fisher, is an educational charity, not a political organisation. It is independent of any political party or group and does not carry on activities intended to affect support for any political party or candidate in any election or referendum, or at any other time. It is financed by sales of publications, conference fees and voluntary donations.

In addition to its main series of publications, the IEA also publishes (jointly with the University of Buckingham) a refereed academic journal, *Economic Affairs*.

The IEA is aided in its work by a distinguished international Academic Advisory Council and an eminent panel of Honorary Fellows. Together with other academics, they review prospective IEA publications, their comments being passed on anonymously to authors. All IEA papers are therefore subject to the same rigorous independent refereeing process as used by leading academic journals.

IEA publications enjoy widespread classroom use and course adoptions in schools and universities. They are also sold throughout the world and often translated/reprinted.

Since 1974 the IEA has helped to create a worldwide network of 100 similar institutions in over 70 countries. They are all independent but share the IEA's mission.

Views expressed in the IEA's publications are those of the authors, not those of the Institute (which has no corporate view), its Managing Trustees, Academic Advisory Council members or senior staff.

Members of the Institute's Academic Advisory Council, Honorary Fellows, Trustees and Staff are listed on the following page.

The Institute gratefully acknowledges financial support for its publications programme and other work from a generous benefaction by the late Professor Ronald Coase.

Other IEA publications

Comprehensive information on other publications and the wider work of the IEA can be found at www.iea.org.uk. To order any publication please see below.

Personal customers

Orders from personal customers should be directed to the IEA:

Clare Rusbridge
IEA
2 Lord North Street
FREEPOST LON10168
London SW1P 3YZ
Tel: 020 7799 8907. Fax: 020 7799 2137
Email: sales@iea.org.uk

Trade customers

All orders from the book trade should be directed to the IEA's distributor:

NBN International (IEA Orders)
Orders Dept.
NBN International
10 Thornbury Road
Plymouth PL6 7PP
Tel: 01752 202301, Fax: 01752 202333
Email: orders@nbninternational.com

IEA subscriptions

The IEA also offers a subscription service to its publications. For a single annual payment (currently £42.00 in the UK), subscribers receive every monograph the IEA publishes. For more information please contact:

Clare Rusbridge
Subscriptions
IEA
2 Lord North Street
FREEPOST LON10168
London SW1P 3YZ
Tel: 020 7799 8907, Fax: 020 7799 2137
Email: crusbridge@iea.org.uk